John Coryton

Stageright

John Coryton

Stageright

ISBN/EAN: 9783337335205

Printed in Europe, USA, Canada, Australia, Japan

Cover: Foto ©Thomas Meinert / pixelio.de

More available books at **www.hansebooks.com**

STAGERIGHT

A COMPENDIUM OF THE LAW RELATING TO

DRAMATIC AUTHORS, MUSICAL COMPOSERS, AND LECTURERS

AS REGARDS THE PUBLIC REPRESENTATION OF THEIR WORKS

With an Appendix

CONTAINING NOTES ON VARIOUS MATTERS CONNECTED WITH THE STAGE, STATUTES
(INCLUDING THE LORD CHAMBERLAIN'S ACT) ETC.

By JOHN CORYTON, Esq.

OF LINCOLN'S INN, BARRISTER-AT-LAW
LATE RECORDER OF MOULMEIN, BRITISH BURMAH
AUTHOR OF 'THE LAW AND PRACTICE OF LETTERS PATENT FOR INVENTIONS'
'THE INDIAN INSOLVENT ACT, WITH NOTES' ETC.

'If the above principles and reasoning are just, why should the Common Law be deemed so narrow and illiberal as not to recognise and receive under its protection a property so circumstanced as the present?'
   per ASTON, J., *Millar* v. *Taylor*, 4 Burr. 2343

'In other matters the [Common] Law has been adapted to the progress of Society according to justice and convenience, and by analogy it should be the same for literary works'
   per ERLE, C.J., *Jeffreys* v. *Boosey*, 4 H. L. Ca. 866

LONDON
D. NUTT, 270 STRAND
1873

CONTENTS.

CHAPTER I.

STAGERIGHT AT THE COMMON LAW.

	PAGE
Nature of Stageright	1
Dramatic Author's right at the Common Law	1
Dramatising a Novel	3
Murray and Elliston	4
Argument in *Murray* v. *Elliston*	6
'Stageright,' origin of the term	9
Common Law right still undetermined	11
Meaning of the expression 'Common Law'	11
Copyright at Common Law	12
Analogy between Stageright and Copyright	21
American Law of Copyright	22
Aston, J., on the Common Law	25
Musical Composers and Lecturers at Common Law	25

CHAPTER II.

BY STATUTE.

Policy of Dramatic Authors before 1833	27
Kept their Plays out of print	27
Early Cases of Stageright	29
Murray v. *Elliston*	33
Legislation on Copyright	33
,, ,, Stageright	36
,, ,, International Copyright and Stageright	39
,, ,, Lectures	47

CHAPTER III.

NATURE OF STAGERIGHT.

	PAGE
Dramatic Piece defined by Statute	50
Place of Dramatic Entertainment	51
Extent to which Authors can control Performances	53
Pantomime is within the Statute	54
Performing immoral pieces	54
Stageright is personalty	56
Titles of plays protected	57
Penalties for infringement are a 'debt' in Bankruptcy	57
Stageright independent of Copyright	57
Consent of Author to performance	58
What is 'Consent in writing?'	59

CHAPTER IV.

PROPRIETOR OF STAGERIGHT.

Author not necessarily the proprietor	60
Principle in *Hatton* v. *Kean*	60
Shepherd v. *Conquest*	61
Wallerstein v. *Herbert*	65
American Law as to proprietorship	65
Joint Authors	66
Disability of alien Authors in England	67
Assignee of the Authors	75
Registration	76
Difference between Stageright and Copyright as regards registration	78
Stageright assets in Bankruptcy	81

CHAPTER V.

INFRINGEMENT.

Mode of determining piracy	81
Matter not suitable for a jury	82
What is piracy?	83
Similarity of plot in itself no indication of piracy	86
Shakspeare's plots not original	86
Registered Titles of Plays	87
Principle on which the Court protects them	87

CHAPTER VI.

PROCEEDINGS AGAINST INFRINGERS.

	PAGE
Statutable remedies	89
Proprietors can either sue for penalties or for an injunction and account	89
Grounds of equitable jurisdiction	89
Ignorance no defence in an action for infringement	92
Bill must state title and shew injury	93
Evidence	94
Presumption from *mala fides*	94
Costs	95

Appendix.

NOTE A. 'The Drama'	i
" B. 'Author's Remedies at Law'	vi
" C. 'Remuneration of Authors'	vii
" D. 'Caricature'	xiii
" E. 'English and French Authors'	xiv
" F. 'Plagiarism'	xvii
STATUTE 3 & 4 Will. IV. c. 15	xx
" 5 & 6 Will. IV. c. 45	xxii
" 5 & 6 Vict. c. 45	xxiv
" 6 & 7 Vict. c. 68	xxxiii
" 7 & 8 Vict. c. 12	xxxix
" 15 & 16 Vict. c. 12	xlvi
ORDER IN COUNCIL, 10 Jan. 1852	li

LIST OF CASES CITED.

Abernethy v. Hutchinson, 47, 50, 54, 98
—— v. Leadbetter, 98
Albert (Prince) v. Strange, 5, 14
Bach v. Longman, 50, 53, 69
Bacon v. Jones, 95
Barfield v. Nicholson, 62, 85
Beckford v. Hood, 4, 19, 76
Bell v. Walker, 85
Blackwell v. Harper, 7
Boosey v. Dalmaine, 86
—— v. Davidson, 97
Boucicault v. Delafield, 71, 100
Bramwell v. Halcomb, 84
Butterworth v. Robinson, 85, 96
Byron v. Johnston, 98
Cambridge University v. Bryer, 20
Carnan v. Bowles, 98
Carr v. Hood, 6
Cary v. Faden, 85
—— v. Longman, 85
Chappell v. Sheard, 90
—— v. Davidson, 90
Clark v. Bishop, 78
Clement v. Maddick, 57, 91
Clementi v. Golding, 55, 65
—— v. Walker, 69, 82
Cocks v. Purday, 70
Colburn v. Simms, 7, 99, 100
Colman v. Wathen, 3, 6, 30
Correspondent Co. (The) v. Saunders 92
Cumberland v. Copeland, 81
—— v. Planché, 57, 79, 80
D'Almaine v. Boosey, 33, 34, 69, 85
Davidson v. Bohn, 82
De Pinha v. Polhill, 84

Doddsley v. Kinnersley, 85
Donaldson v. Beckett, 3, 6, 17, 18, 19
Fitzball v. Brooke, 57
Fradella v. Weller, 99
Gee v. Pritchard, 96
Guichard v. Mori, 39, 70
Gyles v. Wilcox, 7, 83
Hatton v. Kean, 60, 65
Hime v. Dale, 55, 69
Hogg v. Maxwell, 57
—— v. Kirby, 76
Hunt v. Hunt, 56
Jarrold v. Houlston, 89, 98
Jeffreys v. Baldwin, 33, 89
—— v. Boosey, 4, 5, 12, 39, 67, 70, 72
—— v. Bowles, 98
Keene v. Wheatley, 24, 65
Kelly v. Hutton, 91
Lacy v. Rhys, 78, 79
—— v. Toole, 81
Latour v. Bland, 82
Leader v. Purday, 81
Lee v. Simpson, 7, 10, 52, 54, 98
Levi v. Rutley, 66, 81
Lewis v. Fullarton, 89, 98
Longman v. Winchester, 7, 85
—— v. Tripp, 56
Losh v. Hague, 96
Low v. Routledge, 80, 95
Lumley v. Wagner, 67
Lyon v. Knowles, 52, 93
Macklin v. Richardson, 7, 28
Marsh v. Conquest, 2, 56, 58, 80, 93
Matthewson v. Stockdale, 7, 85
Mawman v. Tegg, 8, 82, 92, 94

LIST OF CASES CITED.

Maxwell v. Hogg, 57
Millar v. Taylor, 4, 14, 17, 18, 19, 20, 29, 31, 33
Mirehouse v. Rennell, 11, 12
Moet v. Couston, 100
Morris v. Harris, 31
—— v. Kelly, 31
—— v. Colman, 67
Morton v. Copeland, 58
Murray v. Elliston, 2, 4, 6, 7, 26, 32, 56
Novello v. Sudlow, 51
Page v. Wisden, 94
Palmer v. De Witt, 22, 65
Parsons v. Chapman, 94
Payne v. Moore, 7
Percival v. Phippe, 96
Pike v. Nicholas, 85, 100
Pinnock v. Rose, 85
Planché v. Braham, 7, 52, 53, 84
Pope v. Curl, 35, 49, 50, 54
Power v. Walker, 32, 82
Prince Albert v. Strange, 5, 14
Queensbury (Duke of) v. Shebbeare, 48, 52, 57
Reade v. Conquest, 1, 7, 21, 30
—— v. Lacy, 7, 88
Roper v. Streater, 18, 20
Rundell v. Murray, 82

Russell v. Briant, 52, 93
—— v. Smith, 26, 51, 53, 94
Saunders v. Smith, 92
Sayer v. Dicey, 80
Scott v. Sandford, 90
Seixo v. Provezende, 57
Shepherd v. Conquest, 60, 61, 79
Sheriff v. Coates, 91, 98
Southey v. Sherwood, 52
Stationers' Case, The, 16
Storace v. Longman, 65
Sweet v. Benning, 64
—— v. Cater, 92
—— v. Maugham, 99
Thompson v. Stanhope, 52, 89
Tinsley v. Lacy, 21, 50, 88, 94
Tonson v. Collins, 17, 25, 53, 57
Toole v. Young, 21, 84
Trusler v. Murray, 89, 95
Turner v. Robinson, 5
Upmann v. Elkan, 100
Walcot v. Walker, 54
Wallerstein v. Herbert, 65
Webster v. Dillon, 67
Whittingham v. Wooler, 98
Wilkins v. Aikin, 7, 83
Wood v. Boosey, 58, 80
—— v. Chart, 44, 74, 99
Wyatt v. Burnard, 96

Rights
of
Dramatic &c. Authors.

1. AT THE COMMON LAW.

THE money paid by the public for admission to theatres, operas, lectures, and the like, is the value of certain properties contributed by managers, authors, actors, singers, lecturers, and others. I purpose considering the share of these proceeds to which the dramatic, musical, or literary author is entitled.

And first as to the sole right of representing a drama[1] at Common Law. Whether the author has such a right was a question which was raised, but can hardly be said to have been decided, in the recent case of *Reade* v. *Conquest*.[2]

The declaration[3] in that case contained two counts— 1. That the defendant had acted the plaintiff's play called 'Gold.' 2. That he had acted a play which was virtually plaintiff's novel, 'It is never too Late to Mend;' and that thereby plaintiff had been injured in his sale of the novel, and 'also had been, and was, and would be, wholly prevented from dramatising the said book, novel, and story, and from selling it as dramatised, and from selling or

---

[1] Note A., Appendix, 'The Drama.' [2] 1861, 9 C.B. (N.S.) 755.
[3] Note B., Appendix, 'Author's Remedies at Law.'

letting to managers of theatres and others the right of performing it as dramatised.'

The defendant demurred to the second count, the points marked for argument being:—

1. Copyright is defined by statute to be the sole and exclusive liberty of printing or otherwise multiplying copies of a book, and the right of an author does not extend beyond the rights so defined, 5 & 6 Vic. c. 45, § 1.

2. Piracy, or the infringement of copyright, does not extend beyond illegally printing copies of a book in which there is copyright, or publishing copies illegally printed. § 15.

3. Dramatising a novel is no infringement of copyright. It is no more than reading or reciting in public the novel or parts of it.

A considered judgment was delivered by Williams, J.,[1] who said, 'The second count of the declaration alleged that the plaintiff was the duly registered proprietor of the copyright of a certain registered book, viz. a tale or novel entitled "It is never too Late to Mend," and complained that the defendant, without the plaintiff's consent, dramatised the said novel, and caused it to be publicly represented and performed as a drama at the Grecian Theatre for profit, and thereby the sale of the book[2] was injured, &c. To this count there was a demurrer, and it was insisted on the part of the defendant, that, representing the incidents of a published novel in a dramatic form upon the stage, although done publicly and for profit, is not an infringement of the plaintiff's copyright[3] therein, and we are of opinion that the defendant's contention is correct.

'The right claimed by the plaintiff is twofold. First

[1] The other judges present at the argument were Erle, C.J., and Keating, J.

[2] That this allegation formed the basis of the Court's judgment, I gather from the use of the word *copyright* in its most material passages. See *Marsh* v. *Conquest*, 17 C.B. (N.S.) 418, and the argument in *Murray* v. *Elliston*, 5 B. & Ald., 657, cited *post*, p. 6.

[3] See preceding note.

he contended that his statutable right was infringed by the act of the defendant. It was held, however, in *Colman v. Wathen*, 5 T. R. 245, that representing a public dramatic piece of the plaintiff upon the stage was not a publication within the meaning of the 8 Anne c. 19, so as to subject the defendant to the penalty imposed by the statute, and the sec. 2 of the 5 & 6 Vic. c. 45, defining copyright to mean "the sole and exclusive liberty of printing or otherwise multiplying copies of any subject to which the said word is herein applied," seems to furnish a complete answer to the plaintiff's claim under the statute. Nor, indeed, did he much rely on it. His main reliance was placed on the general ground that even if his statutable right had not been infringed, yet that as an author, he had a copyright[1] at Common Law concurrently with but more extensive than his right under that statute, and that such Common Law right had been invaded by the act of the defendant.

'Now, it is not necessary, in order to decide the present case, to consider the question upon which so much learning has been exhausted, viz. whether anterior to the Statute of Anne, there existed a copyright at Common Law in published books, more extensive in its nature and duration than the right conferred or expressed by that statute. There can, we think, be no doubt that the weight of authority in the time of Lord Mansfield was in favour of the existence of such a right, although the doctrine has found less favour in modern times; but the continued existence of any such right, after the passing of the statute of Anne, was distinctly denied by the majority of the judges in *Donaldson* v. *Beckett*, 4 Burr 2408, 2 Bro. P. C. 129, and the case itself expressly decides that no such right exists after the expiration of the period prescribed by the Act.

'The question therefore seems to us narrowed to this,

---

[1] The word Copyright would seem here to be used precisely in the sense of Stage-right. See Note B., Appendix.

viz., whether the statute of Anne having expressly put an end to such a right if it ever existed after the period it prescribes, has yet preserved it during the currency of such period. That it has done so is a proposition which we think it difficult for the plaintiff to maintain. That a Common Law right of action attaches upon the invasion of the copyright created by statute was decided in the case of *Beckford* v. *Hood* 7 T. R. 620, and followed in several other cases but we are not aware of any case since *Millar* v. *Taylor* 4 Burr. 2303 was overruled by the House of Lords, which decides and recognises that an author of a published work has any other than the statutable copyright therein.

'In the case of *Murray* v. *Elliston* 5 Barn. & Ald. 657 (before the 3 & 4 Will. c. 15), Lord Byron's tragedy of "Marino Faliero," the copyright of which belonged to the plaintiff, had been abridged by curtailing the dialogues and soliloquies, and publicly represented in that form by the defendant at Drury Lane Theatre for profit, the advertisements describing it as Lord Byron's tragedy. A bill for an injunction having been filed, a case was sent for the opinion of the Court of Queen's Bench whether the plaintiff could maintain an action against the defendant under the circumstances. The argument for the plaintiff there was put upon the same ground as in the present case,[1] but the Court certified that no action would lie, a decision which appears in point against the plaintiff upon this record.

'That much might be urged in favour of the Common Law right if the question were *res integra* cannot be doubted by any one who has read the learned judgments of the majority of the Court in *Millar* v. *Taylor* (and on the part of my brother Keating and myself I must be allowed to add) of Mr. Justice Erle in the case of *Jeffreys* v. *Boosey* 4 Ho. of Lds. Ca. 876. But it was the opinion

---

[1] The argument in *Murray* v. *Elliston*, will be found *post*, p. 6.

of a large majority of the judges and law lords in that case that the time had passed when the question was open to discussion, and that it must now be considered to be settled that copyright in a published work only exists by statute.

'The learned counsel for the plaintiff, in his argument, cited a case of *Turner* v. *Robinson* 10 Irish Ch. Rep. 121 (on appeal, p. 510) in which it was supposed that the Master of the Rolls in Ireland had taken a view favourable to the plaintiff's claim in the present case. Upon looking to the report, however, it will be found that the opinion of that learned judge is directly opposed to such a claim. In that case the plaintiff had applied for an injunction to prevent the defendant from pirating an original picture of 'The death of Chatterton,' of which the plaintiff was proprietor, by means of stereoscopic apparatus. The Master of the Rolls being of opinion upon the facts that there had been no publication of the picture, and that the imitation was a piracy, granted the injunction, but his opinion upon the point involved in the claim of the plaintiff upon this record was thus expressed:—"It is not necessary," said that learned judge, "to go through the authorities collected in the cases to which I have referred,[1] as I apprehend it is clear that by the Common Law copyright or protection exists in favour of works of literary art or science to this limited extent only, that while they remain unpublished no person can pirate them, but that after publication they are by Common Law unprotected. There has been much difference of opinion on the subject among the judges in England, but the law is now considered to be as I have stated it." The opinion of the Master of the Rolls in Ireland may therefore be added to the weight of authority in this country in favour of the position, that copyright or protection to the works of

---

[1] *Prince Albert* v. *Strange*, 1 McN. and G. 25 ; 1 Hall and Twells 1 ; *Jeffreys* v. *Boosey*, 4 H. of Lds. Ca. 815.

literature after they have been published exists only by statute.'

Judgment was accordingly given for the defendant.

The case of *Murray* v. *Elliston* has earned for itself so unfortunate a notoriety with reference to Stage-right, that it may be well to see what the argument on which the Court here seems inclined to lay some stress really was. It seems to have very little more than an assertion of Copyright at Common Law, and to be mainly occupied with the damages to which plaintiff's Copyright was exposed by the course taken by the defendant. It is reported as follows :[1]—' *Scarlett* for the plaintiff. " This question is quite different from that in *Colman* v. *Wathen* 5 T. R. 245. There it turned upon the words of the statute, 8 Anne, c. 19, and the point determined was that the acting a piece on the stage was not a publication of it within that statute. Here the question is different, for it depends not on the statute but on the right of property which the plaintiff has in his work. The moment such a right is established the consequences must follow that any injury done to the property is the subject of legal redress. This is the only mode in which it may be injured. Unfair and malicious criticism is another, and for that an action will lie *Carr* v. *Hood*, 1 Camp. 335. Suppose this play failed of success when represented, the sale of the work would thereby be damaged. Besides, the curiosity of the public would be thereby satisfied, and so the plaintiff would be injured in the sale of this work. And whether that right of property arise from the Common Law or from the statutes relative to it is in this case immaterial. For if the statute makes a literary work property, the Common Law will give the remedy for the invasion of it. The only question is whether the representation of this piece for profit may not injure the copyright."' The only other cases cited during the argument were *Donaldson* v. *Beckett* 4 Burr. 2408 ; *Macklin*

[1] 5 B. & Ald. 657.

v. *Richardson* Amb. 694; and *Gyles* v. *Wilcox* 2 Atk. 141.

The Certificate given by the Court in *Murray* v. *Elliston*, was signed by Abbott, Bayley, and Holroyd, J.J. It was unaccompanied by any reasons, and ran thus:—' We have heard the case argued by Counsel, and are of opinion that an action cannot be maintained by the plaintiff against the defendant for publicly acting and representing the said tragedy abridged in manner aforesaid at the Theatre Royal Drury-Lane for profit.'

That the question of Stage-right, pure and simple, and quite apart from the question of copyright, is raised by the pleadings in *Reade* v. *Conquest* (*ubi sup.*) will, I think, be clear from so much of the second count as I have quoted. That the argument at the bar was considered to rest wholly upon this count, I infer from the observations of the Court[1] during the argument.

On a special case[2] arising out of the same matter and between the same parties, Erle, C. J., said ' The plaintiff sued for an alleged infringement of his stage-copyright in a drama called " Gold." The defendant had caused to be represented a drama called " Never too Late to Mend," and it is clear that in so doing he was guilty of the infringement complained of unless the facts mentioned below constitute a defence because many parts of the two dramas were the same, and the 3 & 4 Will. IV., c. 15, § 2, enacts that if any person without the consent of the

---

[1] It was asked by Williams, J., *inter alia*, whether Counsel would contend that the painter of an historical scene could restrain the representation of that scene by *poses plastiques*, a position considered by his lordship to be analogous and suggestive of a *reductio ad absurdum* of the plaintiff's line of argument.

[2] *Reade* v. *Conquest*, 1862, 11 C.B. (N.S.) 479. The case was argued by the plaintiff in person citing *Lee* v. *Simpson*, 3 C.B., 871; *Reade* v. *Lacy*, 30 Law J. Ch. 655; *Blackwell* v. *Harper*, 2 Atk. 95; *Planché* v. *Braham*, 4 N.C. 17, 5 Scott 242, 8 C. and P. 68; and *Colburn* v. *Simms*, 2 Hare, 543. For the defendant were cited *Payne* v. *Moore*, 1 East 361; *Matthewson* v. *Stockdale*, 12 Ves. 270; *Longman* v. *Winchester*, 16 Ves. 269; and *Wilkins* v. *Aikin*, 17 Ves. 422.

proprietor shall represent any dramatic production therein described or any part thereof he shall be liable to a penalty of not less than forty shillings.'

'The facts on which the defendant relied were that the plaintiff had published a novel called "It is Never too Late to Mend," which was the drama called "Gold," presented in the form of a novel, containing as substance the same incidents, and characters, and language, and that the defendant dramatized this novel, calling his drama "Never too Late to Mend," and in so doing took many of the characters and incidents and much of the language of the novel. The consequence was that many parts of the drama "Never too Late to Mend" were the same as the corresponding parts of the drama "Gold." But the brother so composed his drama from the plaintiff's novel without having seen or in any way known of the plaintiff's drama "Gold," and took nothing directly therefrom. The drama so composed by his brother, the defendant represented at his theatre, and on these facts he contended that his brother was the author of the drama so represented by him within the meaning of the Statute 3 & 4 Will. IV. c. 15. If he was the author, it follows that the plaintiff was not, and that no right of the plaintiff has been violated.'

'It was argued for him that copyright differs from patent right in this, that the patent is to the first inventor, and that there cannot be two first inventors, although there may be two original inventors, whereas copyright belongs to the author of the composition, and if two authors invented the same ideas, and clothed them in the same words, each author might have copyright in the same composition, although composed by two original authors. In that case it was contended that neither of the authors would have infringed any of the rights of the other. A party who multiplied copies taken from such a composition as published by one of them might be liable for infringement of copyright to the author from whose publication he had taken the copies, if that was ascertained, without incurring any liability towards the other author. Upon this principle he contended that the defendant's brother was an original author of his drama, "Never too Late to Mend," and had both the book-copyright and the stage-copyright[1] therein.

'The Court has already decided in this case, that the representation of the brother's drama was no infringement of the plaintiff's book-copyright in his novel,[2] and the defendant now further contended that such representation was no infringement of the plaintiff's stage-copyright on his drama called "Gold," because the brother was the author of his drama. But we think that this ground of defence fails. The defendant's brother was not the author of those parts of the drama "Never too Late to Mend," which he copied directly from the plaintiff's novel, and indirectly from the plaintiff's drama "Gold."

'It is not necessary to decide whether, if the brother published his drama, he would infringe the plaintiff's book-copyright under the 5 & 6 Vic. c. 45, in his novel or drama above mentioned. If that question should arise it would then be time to decide whether the defendant could find any defence; but it is clear that he could not in that case defend himself on the ground that he was the author of the parts which he copied. Here the question that arises is in respect of the plaintiff's stage-copyright in his drama "Gold." This copyright, under 3 & 4 Will. IV. c. 15, is infringed if the whole or any part of it should be represented without leave, and it is clear that a very considerable part of it has been represented by the defendant. He is, therefore, liable in this action, unless he has an excuse. The excuse offered is as above stated, that the

---

[1] The word 'Stage-right' (coined, as I understand, by Dr. C. Reade, in 1859) expresses somewhat more accurately the right in question.

[2] See note *ante* p. 2. It would appear from this passage of the judgment that the learned judge's assent to the judgment in the former case was given on the assumption that damage to the copyright, or, as his Lordship here terms it, 'book-copyright,' was not sustained.

brother is the author of these parts. But the fact is not so. . . . . . The fallacy lies in the allegation that the defendant's brother is the author of the drama " Never too Late to Mend," which is true in one sense and untrue in another. He is the author of parts of it, and in respect of publishing, or representing them, he infringes no right of others, and might sue any other who infringed his right. But in respect of the parts copied from the plaintiff, if he was sued for publishing and infringing the book-copyright he might perhaps be excused under some of the rules relating to literary property, and to the power of abridging or taking extracts therefrom, or the like; but he could not justify on the ground that he was the author, and if, as here, he is sued for representing those parts, and so infringing the stage-copyright, he cannot justify as author, and that alone is the ground which is now to be disposed of. The point that the defendant had a defence in his belief that his brother had a right to dramatise the novel, and that therefore he had a right to represent the drama, could not be relied on. If he had the right, his belief would be immaterial. If he had not the right, and had done the wrong complained of, his belief that he was not doing wrong is equally immaterial. In *Lee* v. *Simpson* 3 C. B. 871, 6 D. & L. 666, the defendant had purchased the piece which he represented, and believed he had the right, but on proof by the plaintiff that *he* had the right, the judgment was against the defendant on the ground that he had infringed the plaintiff's property protected by statute, and was an offender within its terms, and if the plaintiff was bound to show the defendant's knowledge the protection awarded by the statute would be illusory.'

The marginal note of this case is that the matter complained of was 'an infringement of the plaintiff's copyright in his drama.' Here, as in the case before referred to, the word is used in the sense of stage-right. I take it that the latter case establishes that, so far as unlicensed representation under stat. 3 & 4 Will. IV. c. 15 is concerned, it is immaterial whether the original which has been pirated is in the form of a novel or a play.

The question whether there was Stage-right at the Common Law is, I apprehend, unsolved by either of these judgments, and it may be well, when considering the matter with reference to rights essentially the creation of modern times, to ascertain clearly what is meant by rights existing at the Common Law. Simple as the subject may appear, it has been productive of much diversity of opinion among the highest authorities of the law.[1] 'Our English lawyers,' observes Hallam ('Middle Ages,' vol. ii. 465), ' prone to magnify the antiquity, like the other merits of their system, are apt to carry up the date of the Common Law till, like the pedigree of an illustrious family, it closes in the obscurity of ancient times; Sir Matthew Hale not hesitating to say that its origin is as undiscoverable as that of the Nile, and Burke, in his " Introduction to English History," remarks on the evil consequences that are to be ascribed to an opinion, which, he says, is hardly to be eradicated from the minds of our lawyers, " that the English law has been formed and grown up among ourselves," is quite peculiar to this island, and has continued in much the same state from an antiquity to which they hardly allow any bounds.' (See Fortescue *de Laudibus Legum Angliæ*, with Notes by Professor Amos, p. 50.)

The following is the language in which Lord Wensleydale, then Mr. Baron Parke, speaks of the Common Law in *Mirehouse* v. *Rennell*, a case on error in the House of Lords, 8 Bing. 515 :—'The precise facts stated by your Lordships have never, as far as we can learn, been adjudicated upon in any Court, nor is there to be found any opinion on them of any of our judges, or of those ancient text-writers to whom we look up as authorities. The case, therefore, is in some sense new, as are many others which continually occur, but we have no right to consider it, because it is new, as one for which the law has not pro-

---

[1] I. Step. ' Bl. Com.' Introd. Sec. III.

vided at all, and because it has not been decided to decide it for ourselves according to our own judgment of what is just and expedient. Our Common Law system consists in applying to new combinations of circumstances those rules of law which we derive from legal principles and judicial precedents, and for the sake of attaining uniformity, consistency, and certainty, we must apply these rules when they are not plainly unreasonable or inconvenient to all cases which arise; and we are not at liberty to reject them and abandon all analogy to them in those to which they have not hitherto been judicially applied, because we think that the rules are not as convenient or reasonable as we ourselves could have devised. It appears to me to be of great importance to keep this principle of decision steadily in view, not merely for the determination of the particular case, but for the interests of law as a science.'

The subject of controversy in *Mirehouse* v. *Rennell*, we may notice, was an advowson, a species of property the incidents of which had at an early age been well defined.

By the Common Law we mean[1] 'those principles, usages, and rules of action applicable to the government and security of person and property which do not rest for their authority upon any express or positive declaration of the will of the Legislature.'

The system of the Common Law, or as Bentham, by a pregnant synonym, has termed it, 'judge-made law,' has rarely received so admirable an exposition with reference to the class of property we are considering as in the opinion delivered by Erle C. J., in *Jeffreys* v. *Boosey* 4 House of Lords Ca. 866. His Lordship there said:—
'With respect to the property of authors in their works at Common Law, as the authorities conflict, I would propose to recur briefly to some first principles relating to the origin and nature of the property, then to answer some objections, and lastly to review the authorities. The origin of the property is in production. As to works of imagina-

[1] Wharton's Law Lex. tit. 'Common Law.'

tion and reasoning, if not of memory, the author may be said to create, and in all departments of mind new books are the products of the labour, skill, and capital of the author. The subject of property is the order of words in the author's composition, not the words themselves, they being analogous to the elements of matter[1] which are not appropriated unless combined, nor the ideas expressed by those words, they existing in the mind alone, which is not capable of appropriation. The nature of the right of an author in his works is analogous to the rights of ownership in other personal property, and is far more extensive than the control of copying after publication in print, which is the limited meaning of copyright in its common acceptation, and which is the right of an author to which the statute of Anne relates. Thus, if after composition the author chooses to keep his writings private, he has the remedies for wrongful abstraction of copies analogous to those of an owner of personalty in the like case. He may prevent publication. He may require back the copies wrongfully made. He may sue for damages if any are sustained, also if the wrongful copies were published abroad, and the books were imported for sale without knowledge of the wrong, still the author's right to his composition would be recognised against the importer, and such sale would be stopped.
. . . . . Again, if an author chooses to impart his manuscripts to others without general publication, he has all the rights for disposing of it incidental to personalty. He may make an assignment, either absolute or qualified, in any degree. He may lend, or let, or give, or sell, any copy of his composition, with or without liberty to transcribe, and if with liberty of transcribing he may fix the number of transcripts which he permits. If he prints for private circulation only, he has still the same rights, and all these rights he may pass to his assignee. About

---

[1] See for parallel reasoning on the subject of Patents for Inventions the cases cited, 'Coryton on Patents,' p. 62–95, Webster P.R. 134, 1 Carpmael, 639.

the rights of the author before publication, at Common Law all are agreed, and the cases on the point are collected in *Prince Albert* v. *Strange*,[1] but the dispute is whether these rights had any continuance after publication until the statute of Anne. I submit the answer should be in the affirmative, both because printing, which is only a mode of copying, and unconnected with the right of copying, has no legal effect upon that right of control over copying which existed while the work was in manuscript, and because it is just to the author, and useful to the community, in order that production should continue to secure the profits of a production to the labour, skill, and capital thus produced it; and this can only be effected by giving property after publication, as the profits on books only then begin to arise.

'Those who object to the author's right at Common Law after publication, rely mainly on three grounds—1. That copyright after publication cannot be the subject of property. 2. That copyright is a privilege of prohibiting others from the exercise of their right of printing, and a monopoly lawful only by statute. 3. That by publication the property of the author is given to the public.

'With respect to the first of these grounds, that copyright cannot be the subject of property inasmuch as it is a mental abstraction too evanescent and fleeting to be property, and as it is a claim to ideas which cannot be identified nor be sued for in trover or trespass, the answer is that the claim is not in ideas but to the order of words, and that this order has a marked identity and a permanent endurance. . . . . The notion of Mr. Justice Yates[2] that nothing is property which cannot be ear-marked and recovered in detenue or trover, may be true in an early stage of society, when property is in its simple form, and the remedies for violation of it also simple; but it is not true in a more civilised state, when the relations of

---

[1] 18 L. J. Ch. 120, 1 McN. and G. 25, and 1 Hall and Twells, 1.
[2] *Millar* v. *Taylor*, 4 Burr. 2303.

life and the interests arising therefrom are complicated. As property must precede the violation of it, so the rights must be instituted before the remedies for the violation of them, and the seeking for the law of the right of property in the law of procedure relating to the remedies is the same mistake as supposing that the mark on the ear of an animal is the cause instead of the consequence of the property therein. The difference in the judgments of Mr. Justice Yates and Lord Mansfield on this point appears to me to be the difference between following precedent in its unimportant forms and in the essential principles. If the precedents in these unimportant forms are to be followed, it is clear there would be no precedent relating to printing before the time of Richard the First, when the Common Law in theory existed, as printing was not known then, and this objection has been made to copyright at Common Law after printing. But if the essential principles for *one* source of property be production, the mode of production is unimportant. The essential principle is applicable alike to the steam and gas appropriated in the nineteenth century and the printing introduced in the fifteenth, and the farmer's produce of the earlier ages. The importance of the interests dependent on words advances with the advance of civilisation. If the growth of the words be traced with respect to the words that make and unmake a simple contract, and with respect to the words that are actionable or justifiable as defamation, and with respect to the words that are indictable as seditious, or blasphemous, it will be thought reasonable that there should be the same growth of the law in respect of the interest connected with the investment of capital in words. In the other matters the law has been adapted to the progress of society according to justice and convenience, and by analogy it should be the same for literary works, and they should become property with all its incidents on the most elementary principles of securing to industry its fruits and to capital its profits.

'With respect to the second objection, that copyright is a privilege of prohibiting others from the exercise of their right of printing, and so a monopoly lawful only by the statute, I submit I have already shown that copyright is a property and not a personal privilege in the nature of a monopoly. I submit also that the notion of all printers having a right to print whatever has been published is, on the same reasoning, a mistake. The supposition of the objector is that there is a demand for books; that the supply is produced by labour, skill, and capital, for the sake of profit; that the profit begins to arise upon the sale of the production, and that as soon as the sale has commenced the law gives to the pirate an equal right to the profits with the producer; in other words, that the law gives up the most important production of industry to spoliation, which seems inconsistent. There is no ground for the assertion that a printer is at liberty to print anything in print. To use the language of the Court in the *Stationers' Case* 1 Mod. 256, he may print all that has been made common but not that which has remained inclosed. Words are free to all. He may print any words that he can compose or get composed, but it does not follow that he may transcribe what another has appropriated. The printer is prohibited from words of blasphemy and sedition for the sake of the public interest; from words of defamation for the sake of character; from the words of the books in the King's copyright by reason of his property therein. The liberty of printing is restricted in all these instances, and the principle of liberty would not be more infringed if the printing was restricted also as to the property of the author. Whether he is so restricted by law is the question in controversy, and to assume that the supposed law would be contrary to lawful liberty and therefore no law, is merely a form of assuming that the question in dispute is answered.

'With respect to the third objection, that by publication the property is given to the public, if it is meant as a fact that the author intends to give it, it is contrary to the truth, for the proprietors of copyright have continuously claimed to keep it. If it is meant that the publication operates in law as a gift to the public, the question is begged, and the reasoning is in a circle. For the question being whether the law protects copyright after publication, the reasoning in law is that the law does not so protect it, because publication operates as a gift to the public, and the reasoning in fact is that the publication must be taken to operate as a gift to the public because after publication the law does not protect copyright. In further support of this view, and for a more full statement of many points here, for the sake of time, merely touched, I would refer to the arguments of Wedderburn against Thurlow in *Tonson* v. *Collins*,[1] and to the judgments of Lord Mansfield,[2] and Aston, and Willes, J.J. against Yates, J., in *Millar* v. *Taylor*, and to the summing up of the argument on this point in *Donaldson* v. *Beckett*.[3] . . . . In all of these cases the governing question was whether authors had a perpetuity of copyright since the statute of Anne? This House decided in the last case that the statute had restricted the right to the terms of years therein mentioned, but it left the question of copyright at Common Law undecided.

'With respect to the authorities, they decidedly preponderate in favour of copyright at Common Law. For those that are prior to Charles II., I refer, for the sake of time, to them as cited in the cases last mentioned. They are not judicial decisions upon the right, but they are to my mind, good evidence that the right was from the beginning of printing known and supported. By 13 & 14 Charles II. c. 33, § 6, the Legislature recognises copyright, as is

[1] 'Why then were patents granted for fourteen years if the author had before a perpetual property? I answer they were additional guards to that property by giving a cumulative remedy for a term of years. A new remedy will not destroy an ancient right.'—Sir W. Bl. 321.
[2] 4 Burr 2303.
[3] 2 Br. P.C. 129.

shown more fully below.; and in 16 Charles II. the Court of Common Pleas adjudged for it, by deciding in *Roper* v. *Streater*[1] that the assignee of the executor of the author had the copyright in the law reports of the author against the law patentee, and although the law patentee succeeded on error, that was by force of his patent over law works, not from the failure of copyright as to other works.

'Also the statute of 8 Anne, c. 19, is to my mind decisive that copyright existed previously thereto, and as it has been understood in an opposite sense, it may not be a waste of time to examine it with attention. So far from creating the copyright as a new right the statute of Anne speaks of authors who have transferred the copies of their books, and of booksellers who have purchased the copies of books in order to print and reprint the same, and if copyright in printed books was before the statute the subject of sale and purchase, it was the subject of property. It also speaks of the then usual manner for ascertaining the title to that property, for it directs " that the title to the copy of books hereafter to be published shall be entered at the Stationers' Company in such manner as hath been usual. . . . ."

'The judges in construing the 8th of Anne, in *Millar* v. *Taylor*, advert to its parliamentary history as brought in to secure copyright, and altered in its progress to destroy it. But without going upon such a ground of construction, it is legitimate to observe from the statute itself that it appears to have proceeded from the conflicting interests of readers and authors. For the clause which has the appearance of promoting the interest of authors by vesting their property in them for a term, and giving them stringent remedies for their protection during that term, contains the expression which was ultimately discovered, after a most remarkable discussion, by the decision of this House in *Donaldson* v. *Beckett*, to have destroyed

[1] Skinner 234, referred to in 4 Burr 2316.

the perpetuity of this property, the clause vesting the property in them for the term " and no longer." This decision created such a sacrifice of the author's interest as I may assume has been thought inconvenient, seeing that the Legislature made one restoration to authors of their property by 54 Geo. III. and another by 5 & 6 Vic.

'Furthermore, all the actions on the case, and all the injunctions for infringements of copyright during the first fourteen years after publication, are authorities for saying that the copyright of authors at Common Law has continued since the statute of Anne no otherwise affected thereby than limited in duration. For if the statute is to be held to create a new right for fourteen years, it created also a new remedy at the same time, and that remedy, according to law, would be the only remedy. And the very narrow point on which the plaintiff succeeded in *Beckford* v. *Hood*,[1] namely, that the new remedies given by the statute do not extend to the second term of fourteen years given to an author, in respect of which that plaintiff sued, would have been of no avail in correct reasoning for the first term of fourteen years.

'In the learned conflict ending with *Donaldson* v. *Beckett* the numbers for copyright at Common Law are in a great majority. Lord Mansfield, Aston and Willes, J. J., against Yates in *Millar* v. *Taylor*, and ten judges against one for copyright at Common Law, and either eight judges against three or seven against four for an action for infringement in *Donaldson* v. *Beckett*. Against copyright at Common Law the sole judgment is that of Yates, J., of which I have before spoken. Lord Kenyon seems to have held this opinion, from some expressions used by him in *Beckford* v. *Hood*. It is true that he gives the author by that judgment the remedy given by the law in respect of a right at Common Law, but he derives the right from the statute of Anne, and thereby the judgment is, I submit, analogous. Lord Ellenborough also seems to have held

---

[1] 7 T.R. 620.

the opinion from some incidental expression in the *Cambridge University* v. *Bryer*.[1] But the latest judgment on the point is that of Lord Mansfield in *Millar* v. *Taylor*, in which he does the service of tracing the law upon the question to its source in the just and useful. And Lord Mansfield's authority in this matter outweighs that of Lords Kenyon and Ellenborough, not only as an elaborate judgment outweighs an extra-judicial expression, but also because these successors of Lord Mansfield appear to me to have turned away from that source of the law to which he habitually resorted with endless benefit to his country.

'It is true that no record of an action on the case for infringement of copyright prior to the statute of Anne has been found, the claim in *Roper* v. *Streater*, though founded on copyright, being in form for a penalty under the Licensing Act. But the absence of resort to that remedy is no presumption against the right to it if no such remedy was needed, or if more convenient remedies existed; and there is no reason for believing that such was the case, for printing, when first introduced, was regulated by the Legislature, and confined in its progress by the powers of the Star Chamber and High Commission Courts, and by Licensing Acts and patents for the sole printing of certain works. And so late as the 13 & 14 Charles II. c. 33, § 11, the number of printers is restricted by that statute to twenty and of typefounders to four; and proprietors of copyright then registered with the Stationers' Company and came under their regulations. And thus the opportunities for piracy were rare, while presses were few and known, and consequently the need of an action on the case against a pirate would be small.

'Furthermore, if there were pirates, the remedies in the Star Chamber and for penalties under the statutes were probably more convenient than actions for damages. Indeed, it is noticed by Willes, J., in *Millar* v. *Taylor*,

[1] 16 East 37.

that in the time of Queen Anne the poverty of those who practised piracy was such as to make an action for damages against them futile, and that therefore the booksellers petitioned for the statute of Anne to enable them to punish piracy by penalty and confiscation. In such a state of society and of the law the absence of an action on the case is of no weight in the way of presumption against the right.

'Upon this review of principle and authority, I submit that authors have property in their works by Common Law as well since the statute of Anne as before it.'

The reasoning in this masterly argument would seem *mutatis mutandis* as applicable to stageright as to copyright, and definitively to establish the right of both to protection at Common Law. I would add to it a word only as to the argument arising out of the special circumstances of the case. The author of a drama, whether in the form of a novel or a play, does, as a fact, create a property which has from the moment of its completion a market value for the theatrical world. Without the assistance of the law he is powerless to secure that value. The law which struggles to find an owner wherever the idea of property is concerned will most certainly adjudge the property to the person that has created it, and give him, in the case of any disturbance in his rights, a remedy based on that *summa ratio* spoken of by Coke,[1] *quæ jubet quæ sunt utilia et necessaria et contraria prohibet.*

The whole question of stageright at the Common Law has quite recently been raised anew and the doctrine laid down in *Reade* v. *Conquest* challenged, in the case of *Toole* v. *Young*[2] in the Queen's Bench. In that case an action was brought for the wrongful representation at a provincial theatre of a play assigned to the plaintiff. In 1863 H. wrote for 'Good Words' a tale called 'Not above

---

[1] Co. Lit. 391. *Tinsley* v. *Lacy*, 1863, 1 H. & M. 747.
[2] Reported in *The Times* and other papers, February 22, 1873.

his Business.' He dramatised the story in 1865, and sold the play to the plaintiff, but the plaintiff neither published nor acted it. In 1872 the defendant played a piece called 'Glory,' which plaintiff alleged to be an infringement of his right.

The question of law raised in this case is still awaiting consideration. Pending its decision I would call attention to a very remarkable case of dramatic copyright, *Palmer* v. *De Witt*,[1] recently decided by the Superior Court of New York, enunciating as it does, either directly or by implication, the following principles:—

1. That the right of an author or his legal representatives to the exclusive use and enjoyment of an unpublished work is perpetual.

2. That this right can only be destroyed or lost by the assent or other dedicatory act of the author or his legal representatives.

3. That this right is property, and as such is capable of assignment either in whole or in part, and that an assignee even for a limited period or place will be subrogated to such rights, and protected.

4. That the alienage of such author is no bar to such rights at Common Law, and will not abridge the remedy of either himself or his assignee for a violation of those rights.

5. That the public scenic representation or performance of an unpublished dramatic work is not a publication of such work either at Common Law or by statute, nor is it any abandonment of any proprietary right ; but that an unauthorised performance of such a drama by others is an invasion of, and an infringement of, those proprietary rights ; and that the unauthorised printing and publishing of such a drama is equally a violation of the author's rights.

6. That no notice of a reservation of proprietary rights

---

[1] Printed case : Diossy and Co., New York. 1871.

is required of the author or literary proprietor of an unpublished work upon its use or public performance.

7. That a spectator or auditor at such public performance cannot write out the words of a play, even from memory, and then sell or make any other use of a copy so obtained.

8. That no presumption arises from the public performance of an unpublished or manuscript drama by its author or his assignee, that such author or assignee intended to part with any of his rights in such drama or its use; nor does any presumption arise that a spectator attending such performances could acquire any rights adverse to the author.

9. That if the author of a play should authorise a performance, the actors could not repeat the performance for their or for any other persons' benefit except by permission of the author. They have been taught their parts for a specific and limited purpose that cannot be extended by themselves.

10. That the Copyright Statutes of England and the United States have neither taken away nor abridged the Common Law rights of authors or of their assigns in unpublished works; nor have those statutes in any way impaired the remedies, equitable and legal, for the infringement of said rights by others.

The following is an extract from Mr. Justice Monell's judgment:[1]—' The value to an author of his literary composition, beyond the fame it secures him, is in the amount of money it returns, and the amount of money he gets depends chiefly upon the appreciation of the public. If a composition never comes to the knowledge of the public its author does not obtain either their applause or money. It might as well never have been created or lie in the author's drawer unread.

' Such is the definition of literary property as given

---

[1] Printed case, p. 18.

in *Keene* v. *Wheatley* (23 L. R. 396): namely, the right which entitles an author or his assignees to all the use and profit of his composition. . . . . If a literary composition therefore derives its value from, and becomes property because of, the use which can be made of it before the public, and such value is increased or diminished in proportion to the extent of its use, then it becomes very important to know where and when the author's literary property in it terminates.

' To give it value or to make it property recognized by the Common Law the author must be allowed to use it before the public; and if having submitted it once to a public hearing is to be deemed a publication so as to take away the proprietary right and to deprive the author of the benefit of copyright laws, then obviously the Common Law means nothing, and there is no such thing as property in literary work. . . . . Can it be said that once delivering a lecture upon a scientific or literary subject before a public audience will for ever therefore deprive the author of his property in the ideas invented or created, and which represent by a combination of words his meaning? If so, then any one who can obtain the manuscript or access to it, or who by employing the art of stenography, or by the exercise of memory, can carry it out of a public lecture-room, may, without the consent or knowledge of the author, appropriate and use for his own emolument the literary production of another person. I cannot believe there is so little foundation for, or so narrow a limit to, the proprietary rights of an author in his literary labours. I believe the law intended to secure to him the beneficial results of his labours, and to protect him from any piratical invasion of his rights until he has done some act inconsistent with an exclusive ownership, and which shall amount in judgment of law to a publication.

' There can be no fixed rule determining when an author has surrendered his literary property. Printing his composition and giving it public circulation would fix the period of surrender in such a case; but one reading of a manuscript lecture or one performance of a manuscript play would not, and if one does not, what greater number can it be said will? The value to the author of a lecture or of a play who derives emolument from its delivery or representation before public audiences is not limited to one performance. It may extend to any greater number, and the hundredth performance may bring more ample returns than the first.'

The more the matter is discussed, the more clearly I think it will be seen that its decision depends wholly upon elementary principles of right and wrong, such as formed the staple of the arguments, both at the bar and on the bench, in the famous case of copyright so often referred to.[1] That an American Court should have been the first to expound those principles aright may not perhaps be flattering to our pride, but we may find consolation in reflecting that the spirit of that judgment has never been wholly absent from our English courts, and we may refer with pride to language such as that held by Aston, J., in the great parallel controversy as to the existence of copyright at Common Law. 'The invasion of this sort of property,' his Lordship said,[2] ' is as much against every man's sense of it as it is against natural reason and moral rectitude. It is against the conviction of every man's own breast who attempts it. He knows it not to be his own. He knows he injures another, and he does not do it for the sake of the public, but *malâ fide* and *animo lucrandi*.

'The artificial reasoning drawn from refined metaphysical speculation is all on that side of the question. It is arguing by analogy only to things of a different nature " that it is not tangible," and the like.

[1] See also the very learned argument of the Solicitor-General in *Tonson v. Collins*, 1 W. Bl. 321, heard before Lord Hardwicke in 1752.
[2] 4 Burr 2343.

'The law of nature and truth and the light of reason and the common sense of mankind is on the other side, for *Jus naturæ propriè est dictamen rectæ rationis quo scimus quid turpe quod honestum quid faciendum quid fugiendum sit.*

'The Common Law, now so called, is founded on the law of nature and reason. Its grounds, maxims, and principles are derived from many fountains, says Judge Dodderidge[1] in his "English Lawyer," from natural and moral philosophy, from the civil and canon law, from logic, from the use, custom, and conversation among men, collected out of the general disposition, nature, and condition of human kind.

'If the above principles and reasoning are just, why should the Common Law be deemed so narrow and illiberal as not to recognise and receive under its protection a property so circumstanced as the present?'

The same observations as are here made with reference to the dramatic author would apply, with little modification, to the rights at Common Law of the musical composer and the lecturer. To use the words of Lord Denman, when discussing the Dramatic Copyright Act, in *Russell* v. *Smith*,[2] 'As there appears no reason for favouring one species of literary property more than another, it is probable that this protection was intended for all productions adapted to this mode of publication.'

II. BY STATUTE.

The decision in *Murray* v. *Elliston,* before mentioned, having drawn attention to the subject,[3] an Act (known as 'Bulwer Lytton's Act' 3 & 4 Will. IV. c. 15) was passed

[1] Doctor and Student.
[2] 1848, 12 Q. B. 237.
[3] Per Denman, C.J., in *Russell* v. *Smith*, 1848, 12 Q. B. 237.

in 1833, giving to dramatic [1] authors the right of controlling the public representation of their works, and prescribing penalties for its infringement.

Before considering in detail the provisions of this Act—an Act as important with reference to stageright as the Statute of Anne was as to copyright—it may be interesting to note the means resorted to by authors of dramatic works previous to the Act for the purpose of securing to themselves the right of representing them.[2] These means, as we shall see, were restricted to the simple expedient, recommended by a sort of traditional policy,[3] of keeping the acting copy, except when the piece was actually being played, in their own hands.

The following interesting note,[4] referring to a period earlier than any of the cases I shall mention, is from the pen of a dramatic writer who has exerted himself greatly on behalf of dramatic authors.

' It was always the interest of the proprietors of a play to keep it out of print. There were two kinds of authors, as there were of actors, the paid authors and the sharing authors, of whom Shakspeare was one and Jonson, on a smaller scale, another. It was not the sharing author's interest to print his play, and the paid author lost the right to print his. The sharing author's parental feeling and *amour propre* made him print eventually, but only

---

[1] As to the protection intended to be afforded to other kinds of literary property adapted to this mode of publication, see the remark of Denman, C.J., *ante*, p. 26.

[2] The earliest instance possibly in which the intervention of the Law was invoked for the purpose of restraining rival performances is one mentioned by Collier in his *Annals of the Stage*, vol. i., p. 17, as having occurred in 1378. In that year the scholars or choristers of St. Paul's presented a petition to Richard II., praying him to prohibit some ignorant persons from acting the history of the Old Testament to the prejudice of the clergy of the Church, who had expended considerable sums for a public representation at the ensuing Christmas of plays founded upon that portion of Scripture.

[3] Note C, Appendix, ' Remuneration of Authors.'

[4] The 'Eighth Commandment,' p. 242, by C. Reade (Trübner, 1860).

when the theatre had worn the play quite out... But the sharing actors, whose vanity sided with their interest, held the *bought plays* tight, and kept them out of print with the keenest jealousy. They kept them under lock and key, they hid them, *they destroyed them.* When all their precautions were outwitted, as happened now and then by double MSS. or short-hand, they applied to some great officer of State to restrain the printing, or they bought the printer off, or grinned and closed their stage-door to the author. This they did to Robert Greene.

'Lent unto Robert Shaw, the 18th March, 1599, to give unto the printer to staye the printing of "Patient Grissell," the sum of xxxxs.'

Robert Shaw was the stage manager (*Henslowe's Diary*, 167). For the printing of bought plays restrained by the Lord Chamberlain, see a MS. in Lord Chamberlain's office, entitled 'Cockpit Places appropried' (cited Prolegomena, III., 158). Nor was this, I think, mere jealousy of the press. Five playgoers out of six could not read, but printing enabled other theatres to play their pieces.[1].. The better the play the less likely were the sharers to let it escape into print. No poet's work, unless he was a sharer, was safe. If Shakspeare had sold his plays out and out to a theatre we should have lost many of them. We *have* lost one or two. What has become of 'Love's Labour's Wonne?'

The case of *Macklin* v. *Richardson*,[2] determined in 1770, is very instructive in this particular, although the question of stageright was not directly involved in its decision. The plaintiff was the author of a farce called 'Love à la Mode,' which was played at various theatres in 1760 and following years, but never without his permission. Plaintiff never printed or published the farce. For the representation of it he was paid 20 and 30 guineas

[1] '.... But any theatre could play a play once printed. This defect in literary property lost us the true text of Shakspeare, and also the text of two hundred good plays at least.'

[2] Ambler 694, Cases in Chancery 341, Lib. Reg. 1770 B. fo. 35.

a night by particular actors for their benefits. When the farce was over, the plaintiff used to take back the copy from the prompter. In 1776 the defendants, the proprietors of 'The Court Miscellany, or Gentleman and Lady's Magazine,' employed one Gurney, a short-hand writer, to go to the playhouse and take down the words of the farce from the mouths of the actors, for which they paid him a guinea. Having so done, and corrected his notes from the memory of the defendant Urquhart, they published in the Miscellany for the month of April, 1766, No. 10, the first act, with the names of the actors, and added a print by way of frontispiece, and titled it 'The First Act of Love à la Mode,' and at the end gave notice that the second act would be published in the next month's Miscellany. The defendants printed 4,500 of the Miscellany for that month, and sold 3,400.

The plaintiff filed a bill for an account of the profits made by the defendants, and to restrain them from printing or publishing the Miscellany so containing the first act of 'Love à la Mode,' and from printing and publishing the second act. The common injunction being obtained till answer, was afterwards continued till hearing. The cause came on to be heard before Lord Camden, but the case of *Millar* v. *Taylor*, relative to literary property, being then depending before the Court of King's Bench, and it not being foreseen how far the determination in that case might affect the present case, his Lordship ordered this cause to stand over till after that other should be determined. The Court of King's Bench having given an opinion, three judges against one, that the author of a book had a property in his work independently of the statute of Anne, the cause came on to be heard. The plaintiff waiving the account, the injunction restraining the defendants from printing and publishing the farce, or any part, was made perpetual, with costs.

The tenour of the argument for the defence in this case is worth noting, it being contended that the representation of the farce upon the stage gave 'a right to any one of the audience to carry away what they could and make any use of it.' Lord Commissioner Smythe, giving judgment, made the following observations:—'It has been argued to be a publication by being acted, and therefore the printing is an injury to the plaintiff; but this is a mistake, for, besides the advantage from the performance, the author has another means of profit from the printing and publishing, and there is as much reason that he should be protected in that right as any other author.' The *dictum* is notable also as implying that even thus early stageright and copyright were recognised by the Court as correlative rights in the author of a dramatic work.

The case of *Colman* v. *Wathen*,[1] by which the Court seems to have been much guided in *Reade* v. *Conquest*, was decided in 1793. I subjoin the report *verbatim*, and from this it will be seen that so far as stageright is concerned it is no decision at all.[2]

'This was an action for the penalty under the statute 8 Anne, c. 19, for publishing an entertainment called "The Agreeable Surprise." The plaintiff had purchased the copyright from O'Keefe, the author, and the only evidence of publication by the defendant was the representation of the piece upon his stage at Richmond. A verdict was taken for the plaintiff with nominal damages, in order to raise the question whether this mode of publication were within the statute. *Law* having obtained a rule for setting aside the verdict, *Erskine* showed cause on the ground that this was sufficient evidence for the jury to conclude that the work had been pirated, for it could not

---

[1] 5 T.R. 245. See 5 and 6 Vic., c. 45, s. 20.

[2] The marginal note of this case is as follows:—'Evidence that the defendant acted the piece on the stage of which (*sic*) the plaintiff had bought the copyright, is not evidence of publication by the defendant within the meaning of the statute 8 Anne, c. 19.'

be supposed that the performers could by any other means have exhibited so perfect a representation of the work. Besides, if this were not held to be a publication within the statute, all dramatic works might be pirated with impunity, and as this was the most valuable mode of profiting by them, and in *Millar* v. *Taylor* 4 Burr 2303, a majority of the judges were of opinion in the House of Lords that an author had an exclusive property in his works, independently of the statute of Anne. Law *contrà* was stopped by the Court.

"Lord Kenyon, C. J.—There is no evidence to support the action in this case. The statute for the protection of copyright only extends to prohibit the publication of the book itself by any other than the author or lawful assignee. It was so held in the great copyright case by the House of Lords, but here was no publication.

'Buller, J.—Reporting anything from memory can never be a publication within the statute. Some instances of strength of memory are very surprising, but the mere act of repeating such a performance cannot be left as evidence to the jury that the defendant had pirated the work itself. Rule refused.'

The next reported case, *Morris* v. *Kelly*,[1] occurred in 1820. It marks a very important advance in the desire of the Courts to protect stageright. The following is the report of the case:[2]—

'This was an application for an injunction upon affidavit and certificate of bill filed to restrain the defendants, Maria Kelly and Arnold, from performing a comedy called "The Young Quaker," written by John O'Keefe, Esq.

---

[1] A case *Morris* v. *Harris* in 1814 is mentioned in Godson on Patents, 390, but is not reported.

[2] 1 J. and W. 481. The marginal note of the case is as follows:—'Injunction granted to restrain the performance of a comedy, the copyright of which had been sold by the author, and had been afterwards assigned by writing to the plaintiffs, although it did not appear whether the original assignment was in writing.'

'The bill and affidavit stated that the copyright of this and other works had been sold between the years 1781 and 1785 by the author, who was still living, to the proprietors of the Haymarket Theatre, and that this theatre and the copyright of all the above works, had been afterwards purchased by, and had been vested in, the plaintiffs. It also appeared that the author, in an address prefixed to a collection of his writings, published several years since, expressed his regret that an inconsiderate disposal of these works prevented their appearance in that publication. It was further stated that the defendant Kelly had published an advertisement announcing the intended performance of the above comedy for her benefit on the 26th June, at the English Opera House, and that the other defendant was the sole proprietor of that theatre.

'*Mr. Heald* and *Sir G. Hampson* in support of the motion.

'The Lord Chancellor: Does the bill state the assignment of the copyright was in writing? The Court of King's Bench has decided that copyright cannot pass, except by writing.[1] Take the injunction upon producing an affidavit of that fact.

'June 22. The plaintiffs were unable to state whether the assignment from the author was in writing, but produced an affidavit that all the MSS. of dramatic compositions belonging to the Haymarket Theatre, including "The Young Quaker," had been assigned to them by these several indentures in writing, dated in the years 1805, 1808, and 1819.

'The Lord Chancellor: I shall assume that your title is regular until they show the contrary.

'Injunction granted.'

These are almost the only cases of stageright to be found in the reports of a date earlier than that of *Murray*

---

[1] *Power* v. *Walker*, 1814, 3 Mau. and Sel. 7.

v. *Elliston*, which, as we have seen,[1] declared the author of a dramatic piece, so far as his control over its representation was concerned, *hors la loi*. They show how vague were the notions prevailing, both in the mind of the public and on the Bench, of the nature of stageright, and the lamentable inability that existed to discriminate between that and copyright.

The legislation that ensued with reference to stageright is so mixed up with that of copyright[2] as to render it advisable, before we consider the statute law of stageright in detail, to glance at the general legislation connected with copyright, beginning with the famous statute 8 Anne, c. 19,[3] (A.D. 1709).

This Act, called by Lord Hardwicke 'a standing patent for authors,'[4] and spoken of by Lord Lyndhurst[5] as 'one of the most laboriously considered Acts that ever passed the Legislature,' is entitled 'An Act for the Encouragement of Learning, by vesting the copies of printed books in the authors or purchasers of such copies during the time therein mentioned.' It was passed at the instance of various booksellers, who had been petitioning Parliament since 1703,[6] and afforded work to several committees, among the members of which were Addison, Steele,

---

[1] *Ante*, p. 4.

[2] 'Copyright,' or as it was formerly termed 'copy,' is defined by Lord Mansfield in *Millar* v. *Taylor*, 4 Burr 2396, as 'a term used for ages to signify an incorporeal right to the sole printing and publishing of somewhat intellectual communicated by letters.' The definition given by 5 & 6 Vic.; c. 45, s. 2, is 'the sole and exclusive right of printing or otherwise multiplying copies' of any subject to which the word is applied in that Act.

[3] Thus ordinarily cited (Ruffhead). It is cited as c. 21 in the edition of the statutes printed by the Record Commission.

[4] The statute was framed for the encouragement of genius and art, and 'in that respect like the statute of new inventions from whence it was taken,' per Hardwicke, C., *Jeffreys* v. *Baldwin*, Amb. 163.

[5] *D'Almaine* v. *Boosey*, 1 Y. & C. Eq. Ex. 299. See also *Jeffreys* v. *Baldwin*, Amb. 163.

[6] The Bill (brought in January 11, 1709) was entitled 'A Bill for securing the property of copies of books to their rightful owners.' Per Willes, J. *Millar* v. *Taylor* (*ubi. sup.*).

and Wortley.[1] The following is an outline of its provisions.[2]

After reciting that 'printers, booksellers, and other persons have of late frequently taken the liberty of printing, re-printing, and publishing, and causing to be printed, re-printed, and published, books and other writings, without the consent of the authors or proprietors[3] of such books and writings,' it enacts (§ 1) that the author of any book or books already printed, who has not parted with his copyright, or the bookseller or other person who may have purchased or acquired the copyright 'shall have the sole right and liberty of printing such book and books for the term of one and twenty years, to commence from the 10th day of April, 1710, and no longer; and that the author of any book or books already composed, and not printed and published, or that shall hereafter be composed, and his assignee or assigns, shall have the sole liberty of printing and re-printing such book and books for the term of fourteen years, to commence from the day of first publishing the same, and no longer.' Booksellers and others infringing the Act are to forfeit pirated copies to 'the proprietor or proprietors of the copy thereof, who shall forthwith damask and make waste paper of them,' and pay a penalty of a penny a sheet for every sheet found in the offender's possession. The Act gives no action for damages. Copies of books are (§ 2) to be entered before publication in the Register-book of the Company of Stationers. After the 25th March, 1710, if (§ 4) any bookseller or printer sells or exposes for sale any book ' at such a price or rate as shall be conceived by any person or persons to be too high or unreasonable,' the Archbishop of Canterbury, the Chancellor or Lord Keeper, the Bishop of London, two

[1] Per Lyndhurst, C.B.; *D'Almaine* v. *Boosey* (*ubi. sup.*).

[2] The Act is repealed, together with the statutes altering and enlarging it, by 5 & 6 Vic. c. 45, s. 1.

[3] This preamble has been cited as evidence that copyright existed at Common Law, and that the statute was intended only to give additional remedies for a limited term. See *ante*, p. 17, note 1.

Chief Justices, Chief Baron, &c., are to settle the prices, and if the price is reduced may order the bookseller to pay costs to the party complaining.[1] The last section of the Act[2] provides that 'after the expiration of the said term of fourteen years the sole right of printing or disposing of copies shall return to the authors thereof, if they are then living, for another term of fourteen years.'

The re-printing in England of books subject to copyright was provided against by the statute of Anne, but the importation of copies printed abroad was not.[3] This omission was remedied by 12 Geo. II. c. 36, on the ground that 'the importation of books from abroad diminishes the revenue and discourages the trade and manufacture of the kingdom.'

Stat. 41 Geo. III. c. 107, passed in the session following the Union with Ireland, extended the statute of Anne to that country, giving the author a special action on the case for damages, and double costs. It further increased the penalty to threepence.

By 54 Geo. III. c. 156 (repealed by the recent Act 5 and 6 Vic. c. 45), some of the subsidiary clauses of the preceding Acts were varied, and the term of copyright extended to twenty-eight years from the day of publication, and if the author should be living at the end of that period, then for the residue of his life.

Other compositions, such as engravings, etchings, prints, maps, charts, and sculpture, have since received from statute protection analogous to that extended to literature. Engravings and prints are protected by 8 Geo. II. c. 13, 7 Geo. III. c. 38, 17 Geo. III. c. 57, 6 & 7 Wm. IV. c. 59, 10 & 11 Vic. c. 95; sculptures, models, and casts, by 38 Geo. III. cc. 71 & 54, Geo. III. c. 56; and

---

[1] This clause is repealed by 12 Geo. II. c. 36.

[2] As to the delivery of copies for the use of universities, &c., prescribed by this Act, see 15 Geo. III. c. 53.

[3] It seems that Ireland before the Union would not have been allowed to be used as a means of piracy in England. *Pope* v. *Curl*, 2 Atk. 342.

designs, whether of ornament or utility[1], by 5 & 6 Vic. c. 100 (amended by 21 & 22 Vic. c. 70), 6 & 7 Vic. c. 65, 13 & 14 Vic. c. 104, 14 & 15 Vic. c. 8, 15 & 16 Vic. c. 6, and 25 & 26 Vic. c. 68.

The first occasion on which the Legislature dealt with stageright was, as has already been observed, in enacting 3 & 4 Will. IV. c. 15, and considering the views prevalent in many quarters on the subject of the stage in former times and the liberal spirit in which that Act is conceived, it is perhaps fortunate for dramatic authors that their interests were not earlier subject to parliamentary supervision. The preamble of the statute of Anne gives an uneasy impression that the interests of authors of other than 'useful books,' might have had less regard paid to them; while from the preamble to the Lord Chamberlain's Act, entitled 'An Act for Regulating Theatres,' 6 & 7 Vic. c. 68,[2] we learn that it was left for that statute to repeal 'An Act passed in the Tenth year of the Reign of King George the Second,[3] intituled ' An Act to Amend so much of an Act made in the Twelfth Year of Queen Anne,[4] intituled An Act for Reducing the laws relating to Rogues, Vagabonds, Sturdy Beggars, and Vagrants into one Act of Parliament; *and sending them whither they ought to be sent,* as relates to common players of interludes.'

Statute 3 & 4 Will. IV. c. 15, entitled 'An Act to Amend the Laws relating to Dramatic Literary Property,' after reciting the general Copyright Act, 54 Geo. III. c. 156, enacts (§ 1) that after the passing of the Act 'the author of any tragedy, comedy, play, opera, farce, or any other dramatic piece or entertainment, composed and not printed and published by the

---

[1] I omit any precise notice of the Acts relating to the printing of linen, cotton, or other fabrics, some of which by including the subject of designs approach closely to the subject of designs protected by these Acts.

[2] Appendix. 'Statutes.'

[3] 10 Geo. II. c. 28.

[4] 12 Anne, s. 2, c. 23, in the ordinary edition. 13 Anne, c. 13, as printed by the Record Commission.

author thereof, or the assignee of such author, shall have as his own property the sole liberty of representing or causing to be represented, at any place or places of dramatic entertainment,' in any part of the British dominions, any such production, 'not printed and published by the author thereof or his assignee, and shall be deemed and taken to be the proprietor thereof, and that the author of any such production printed and published within ten years before the passing of this Act by the author thereof or his assignee, or which shall hereafter be so printed and published, or the assignee of such author shall, from the time of passing this Act or from the time of such publication respectively, until the end of twenty-eight years from the day of such first publication of the same; and also, if the author or authors, or the survivor of the authors, shall be living at the end of that period, during the residue of his natural life, have as his own property the sole liberty of representing or causing to be represented the same at any such place of dramatic entertainment as aforesaid, and shall be deemed and taken to be the proprietor thereof.' Nothing in the Act was to affect any right or authority conferred by the author or his assigns previously to the passing of the Act, but the right of the author or his assigns was to be subject to such right or authority.

Sec. 2 subjects the infringer of the proprietary right to a penalty payable to the proprietor for each and every representation of not less than forty shillings, or 'the full amount of the benefit or advantage arising from such representation, or the injury or loss sustained by the plaintiff therefrom, whichever shall be the greater damages,' together with double costs.

Sec. 3 provides that all actions and proceedings for infringement shall be brought within twelve calendar months next after the commission of the offence.

The most important alteration in 3 & 4 Will. c. 15, was that effected by 5 & 6 Vic. c. 45[1] (known as 'Serjeant

[1] Extended to British Colonies by 10 & 11 Vic. c. 95.

Talfourd's Act'), by sec. 20 of which the provisions of the former Act are extended to musical compositions, the term of protection for both, and the rules as to property and registration being made the same as that prescribed for copyright in books; the first public representation or performance of any dramatic piece or musical composition being deemed equivalent in the construction of the Act to the first publication of any book. In the case of any dramatic piece or musical composition in manuscript, it is declared sufficient for the proprietor of the right to register only 'the title thereof, the name and abode of the author or composer thereof, the name and place of abode of the proprietor thereof, and the time and place of its first representation or performance.'

By sec. 21 of the same Act the proprietors are declared entitled to all the remedies given by the 3 & 4 Will. IV. c. 15, as though incorporated with the said Act.

By sec. 22 it is enacted that no assignment of any book consisting of or containing a dramatic piece or musical composition should be held to convey to the assignee the right of representing or performing such dramatic piece or musical composition, unless an entry made of such assignment in the Registry book expressed the intention of the parties that such right should pass by such assignment.

Sec. 24 declares that no proprietor of copyright in any book published after the passing of the Act should take proceedings for its infringement, without having first made an entry in the book of Registry of the Stationers' Company, in accordance with the requirements of the Act. The omission to make such entry was declared not to affect 'the copyright in any book;' but only the right to sue or proceed in respect of the infringement thereof as aforesaid. 'Provided also that nothing herein contained shall prejudice the remedies which the proprietor of the sole liberty of representing any dramatic piece shall have by virtue of 3 & 4 Will. IV. c. 15, ' or of this Act, *although no entry shall be made* in the book of Registry aforesaid.'

Sec. 25 declares copyright to be personal property, transmissible by bequest, and subject, in case of intestacy, to the same law of distribution as other personal property, and in Scotland to be personal and moveable estate.

We now come to a very interesting change in the status of authors generally. Some time previous to the period we have reached, public attention had been directed to the grievous injuries inflicted on authors by acts of international piracy, and an attempt had already been made to provide a remedy. Without the protection of international law, the production of an author became, as it were, *feræ naturæ* beyond the limits of his country—liable to be diverted to the use of any one choosing to appropriate it. In what light the foreigner was regarded in this country, independently of such protection, those curious in such matters may form a judgment from the elaborate decision given by the judges in the case of *Jeffreys* v. *Boosey* [1] before referred to.

The first legislative effort at the establishment of this species of protection was made in 1838 by the enactment of 1 & 2 Vic. c. 59.[2] By that Act it was provided that the Crown might, by Order in Council, give to books, prints, music, and similar articles from foreign countries the same privileges of copyright as were enjoyed in this country, provided those foreign countries conceded reciprocal privileges. The Act related only to copyright proper, that is, literary copyright; but its important operation was soon extended to stageright, albeit (save by a lamentable circumlocution ' the sole right of representing dramatic pieces or performing musical compositions') that right was left destitute of a name.

On the repeal of 1 & 2 Vic. c. 59, the power of the Crown for entering into negociations with foreign States for securing international law was defined by 7 & 8 Vic.

---

[1] 4 H. of L. Cas. 866. In the Exchequer Chamber 20 L. J. Ex. 354, *Guichard* v. *Mori*, 1831, 9 L. J. Ch. 227.

[2] Repealed by 7 & 8 Vic. c. 12.

c. 12 and 15 Vic. c. 12. The former of these Acts, entitled 'An Act to amend the Law relating to International Copyright,' was passed on the 10th May, 1844.

After reciting 1 & 2 Vic. c. 59 ('The International Copyright Act'), 5 & 6 Vic. c. 45 ('The Copyright Amendment Act'), 3 & 4 Will. IV, c. 15 ('The Dramatic Copyright Act'), statutes 8 Geo. II. c. 13, 7 Geo. III. c. 38, 17 Geo. III. c. 57, and 6 & 7 Will. IV. c. 59 (relating to prints and engravings), and statutes 38 Geo. III. c. 7, and 54 Geo. III. c. 56 (relating to models and busts), the preamble of the Act proceeds, ' And whereas the powers vested in Her Majesty by the said International Copyright Act are insufficient to enable Her Majesty to confer upon authors of books first published in foreign countries copyright of the like duration, and with the like remedies for the infringement thereof which are conferred and provided by the said "Copyright Amendment Act," with respect to authors of books first published in the British Dominions, and the said "International Copyright Act" does not empower Her Majesty to confer any exclusive right of representation or performing dramatic pieces or musical compositions first published in foreign countries upon the authors thereof, nor to extend the privilege of copyright to prints and sculptures first published abroad, and it is expedient to vest increased powers in Her Majesty in this respect, and for that purpose to repeal the said "International Copyright Act," and to give such other powers to Her Majesty, and to make such further provisions as are hereinafter contained," the Act repeals (sec. 1) the 'International Copyright Act.'

Sec. 2 enacts that Her Majesty may by an Order in Council direct, that as regards all or any particular class of the following works, viz. books, prints, articles of sculpture, and other works of art to be defined in such Order, which shall, after a future time to be specified in the Order, be first published in any foreign country named in the Order, the authors and inventors, designers, engravers, and makers of the works respectively, and their executors, administrators, and assigns shall have a copyright in their works for a period defined in the Order, not exceeding, however, the term of copyright which authors, inventors, designers, engravers, and makers of the like works are respectively entitled to when published in this country.

Sec. 3 provides that if the Order in Council applies to books, the Copyright Law as to books first published in this country shall apply to the books to which the Order relates, with certain exceptions, one of which is as to the direct delivery of copies to the British Museum and other libraries.

Sec. 4 provides, as to engraving and sculpture copyright, that if the Order applies to prints, sculptures, or any of the other works of art mentioned above, the copyright law as to prints, sculptures, and works of art first published in this country shall apply to the prints, sculptures, and works of art to which the Order relates.

Sec. 5, as to musical and dramatic copyright, provides that Her Majesty may by an Order in Council direct, that authors and composers of dramatic pieces and musical compositions first publicly represented and performed in foreign countries, may have the sole liberty of representation and performance, and rights of protection, in the same manner as authors of similar works in this country, during a term mentioned in the Order, not exceeding the period given under the copyright, dramatic, and other acts to a similar production here.

Secs. 6–9 provide for the registration at Stationers' Hall, in the case of dramatic and musical compositions, of the title of the same, the name and place of abode of the author or composer, the name and place of abode of the proprietor of the right of representing and performing the same, and the time and place of the first representation or performance in the country named in the Order of Council, and other similar matters.

Sec. 10 prohibits the importation without the registered

proprietor's consent of all copies of works having copyright under this Act, printed in foreign countries other than the country where such works were first published.

Sec. 11 directs the officers of the Stationers' Company to deposit the copies they receive at the British Museum.

Sec. 12 provides that copies of second or subsequent editions need not be delivered to the Stationers' Company unless they contain alterations or additions.

Secs. 13, 14, 15, 16, & 17 relate to the extent and power of the Orders of Council, which, when published in the *London Gazette*, are to have the same effect as if they were part of the Act.

Sec. 18 makes an exception[1] as to translations.

Sec. 19 declares that neither the author of any book, nor the author or composer of any dramatic piece or musical composition, nor the inventor, designer, or engraver of prints, nor the maker of any article of sculpture or of such other work of art as aforesaid, which shall after the passing of this Act be first published out of Her Majesty's dominions shall have any copyright therein respectively, or any exclusive right to the public representation or performance thereof, otherwise than such (if any) as he may become entitled to under this Act.

Sec. 20 is an interpretation section.

In 1851, Conventions having already been entered into under the Act with Prussia, Saxony, and several minor continental states, it was found[2] in the course of arranging a Convention with France that the powers of the Crown as regarded these international engagements required extension.

The Convention with France was signed at Paris on

---

[1] This section has been repealed by s. 1 15 Vic. c. 12, so far as it is inconsistent with that statute. It enacted that nothing in this Act should be construed to prevent the printing, publication, or sale of any translation of any book, the author whereof and his assigns might be entitled to the benefit of the Act.

[2] As to the grounds for passing the amending Act 15 & 16 Vic. c 12, see the speech made by Mr. Labouchere in introducing the Bill. *Hans. Parl. Deb.* vol. cxix. p. 498.

November 3, 1851, Lord Normanby acting as the English and M. Turgot as the French plenipotentiary. It guarantees [1] (Art. 1) equal rights to the authors of the respective countries as to 'works of literature,' which are understood to comprehend books, dramatic works, musical compositions, drawings, paintings, sculptures, engravings, lithographs, and 'any other works whatsoever of literature and the fine arts.'

By Art. 2 the protection granted to original works is extended to translations, 'it being, however, clearly understood that protection is afforded simply to a translator in respect of his own translation, and not to confer the exclusive right of translating upon the first translator of any work except as provided in the next Article.'

Art. 3. 'If the author of any work published in either country wishes to reserve to himself the exclusive right of translating his work in the other country, he may do so for five years from the first publication of the translation authorised by him,' provided (1) the original work is registered and deposited in the one country within three months after the publication in the other; (2) the author notifies on the title-page of his work his intention to reserve the right of translation. (3.) At least a part of the authorised translation appears within a year after the registration and deposit of the original, and the whole is published within three years after the date of such deposit; and (4) the authorised translation appears in one of the two countries, and is registered and deposited in the same way and within the same time as an original book.

By Art. 4 the stipulations of the preceding Articles are declared 'applicable to the representation of dramatic works and to the performance of musical compositions in

---

[1] The full text of this important treaty is given in English and French by Burke "On International Copyright." The English version will be found *post*, in the Appendix. A curious speculation as to the effect upon English law of the very liberal doctrines prevalent in French law as to alien authors will be found (reprinted from the *Athenæum*) in 1 Jur. N.S. pt. II. 523. See Note F Appendix, 'French and English Authors.'

so far as the laws of each of the two countries are or shall be applicable in this respect to dramatic and musical works first publicly represented or performed therein.

'In order, however, to entitle the author to legal protection in regard to the translation of a dramatic work, such translation must appear within three months after the registration and deposit of the original.[1]

'It is understood that the protection stipulated by the present Article is not intended to prohibit fair imitations or adaptations of dramatic works to the stage in England and France respectively, but is only meant to prevent piratical translations. The question whether a work is an imitation or a piracy shall in all cases be decided by the courts of justice of the respective countries according to the laws in force in each.'

Art. 5 permits translations from newspapers under certain restrictions.

Arts. 6, 7 prohibit under penalties the importation of pirated copies of works protected.

Art. 8 prescribes the mode of registration which is compulsory. If the work appears first in France it must be registered at Stationers' Hall, if in the British dominions at the *Bureau de la Librairie du Ministère de l'Intérieur* at Paris.

The Convention then provides for deposit at the British Museum and the National Library in Paris of the works protected. In every case the deposit must be within three months of the first publication. A certificate stating the date of registration is to be given, if required, on payment of certain fees.

By Art. 11 the high contracting powers 'engage to communicate to each other the laws and regulations which may hereafter be established in their respective territories with reference to copyright in works or production' protected by the Convention.

Art. 12 reserves to either State the right of controlling

[1] *Wood* v. *Chart*, 1870, 10 L.R. Eq. 204, 22 L.T., N.S. 432, 9 L.J., Ch. 641.

or of prohibiting by measures of legislation or of internal policy the sale, circulation, representation, or exhibition of any work or production in respect to which either country may deem it expedient to exercise that right.

Art. 13 reserves to either State the right to prohibit the importation into its own dominions of such books as by its internal law or under engagements with other States are or may be declared to be piracies or infringement of copyright.

Art. 14 stipulates that Her Majesty shall recommend Parliament to pass an Act to enable her to carry out the Convention, the period of which it fixes at ten years from the day on which it shall come into operation, or for a further period terminable with a year's notice on either side. The Convention reserves the power of 'making by common consent in this Convention any modifications which may not be inconsistent with its spirit and principles, and which experience of its working may show to be desirable.'

Ratifications were exchanged at Paris on January 8th, 1852. The *procès verbal* of the exchange provides for the immediate execution of so much of the Convention as requires no further sanction of the English law, and makes an alteration with regard to political articles in newspapers.

Act 15 & 16 Vic. c. 12, conferring the required powers on the Crown, and prescribing the conditions to be observed by persons desirous of obtaining the benefit of the Convention, was passed on May 28, 1852. After repealing, by its first section, the 18th section of 7 & 8 Vic. c. 12, 'so far as the same is inconsistent with the provisions hereinafter contained,' the Act empowers Her Majesty, (sec. 2,) by Order in Council, to direct that authors of books published in foreign countries may, for a limited time, prevent unauthorized translations, and (sec. 3) that thereupon the law of copyright shall extend to prevent such translations. By sec. 4 'Her Majesty may, by Order in Council, direct that authors of dramatic pieces, which are after a future time to be specified in such Order, first publicly represented in any foreign country to be named in such Order, their executors, administrators, and assigns shall, subject to the provisions hereinafter mentioned or referred to, be empowered to prevent the representation in the British dominions of any translation of such dramatic pieces not authorised by them, for such time as may be specified in such Order, not extending beyond the expiration of five years from the time at which the authorised translations of such dramatic pieces hereinafter mentioned are first published or publicly represented.'

By sec. 5 it is declared that, 'subject to any provisions or qualifications contained in such last-mentioned Order, and to the provisions hereinafter contained or referred to, the laws and enactments for the time being in force for ensuring to the author of any dramatic piece first publicly represented in the British dominions the sole liberty of representing the same, shall be applied for the purpose of preventing the representation of any translations of the dramatic pieces to which such last mentioned Order extends, which are not sanctioned by the authors thereof.'

Sec. 6, embodying the provision of Art. 4 of the Convention, is most important. It provides that 'nothing herein contained shall be so construed as to prevent fair imitations or adaptations to the English stage of any dramatic pieces or musical composition published in any foreign country.'

Sec. 8 embodies, in the form of an enactment, the provisions of the Convention above referred to as to registration and deposit of copies.

The provisions of this Act are by sec. 10 declared to be incorporated with the International Copyright Act, and construed and read as one with it.

An Order in Council dated January 10, issued on January 20, 1852, specifies the time from which the provisions of the Convention shall take effect. The date specified is January 17, 1852.

The following[1] are the other countries with which similar conventions exist, the date on which the convention was made, and the number of months within which registration and delivery of copies is required:—

Prussia, Saxony, Saxe-Weimar, Saxe-Meiningen, Saxe-Altenburg, Saxe-Coburg-Gotha, Brunswick, Schwarzburg Rudolstadt, Schwarzburg Londerhausen, and Reuss in 1846, with twelve months for registration.

Thuringia, Hanover, Oldenburg, 1847, twelve; Anhalt, 1853, twelve; Hamburg, 1853, three; Belgium, 1855, three; Spain, 1857, three; Sardinia, 1857, three; Hesse-Darmstadt, 1862, twelve.

The right acquired by the composer of a lecture so far as regards its representation is, in some of its phases, similar to that of stageright. Of the position of the public lecturer before the passing of the Statute 5 & 6 Will. IV. c. 65, we may judge from the case of *Abernethy* v. *Hutchinson*,[2] decided by Lord Eldon in 1824. The plaintiff, the celebrated surgeon, delivered a course of lectures to the students of St. Bartholomew's Hospital, some of which were printed without his consent by the *Lancet* newspaper, the editor announcing his intention of publishing others as they were delivered. The plaintiff admitted that the specific matter he delivered had not been previously reduced to writing, although a good deal of the materials for his lectures had been. The case decided (1) that a person who attends oral lectures is not justified in publishing them for profit, and an action at law will lie upon the implied contract by the lecturer against a pupil attending oral lectures, who causes them to be published for profit, and (2) that an injunction will be granted against third persons publishing lectures orally delivered, who have procured the

[1] I give this from Shortt on Copyright, 147.
[2] 3 L.J., 209 Ch., reprinted I.H. and T. 39.

means of publishing those lectures from parties who attended the oral delivery of them, and were bound by the implied contract.

His lordship, in giving judgment, said:—

'There is another ground for an injunction arising out of an *implied contract*. I should be very sorry if I thought that anything which has fallen from me should be considered to go the length of this—that persons who attend lectures or sermons, and take notes, are to be at liberty to carry into print those notes for their own profit, or for the *profit of others*. I have very little difficulty upon that point, but that doctrine must apply either to contract or breach of trust. Now, with respect to contract, it is quite competent for Mr. Abernethy, and for every other lecturer, to protect himself in future against what is complained of here. There is a contract expressed, and a contract implied, and I should be very sorry to have any man understand that this Court would not act as well upon a contract implied as upon a contract expressed, provided only the circumstances of the case authorise the Court to act upon it. I have not the slightest difficulty in my own mind that a lecturer may say to those who hear him, "You are entitled to take notes for your own use, and to use them, perhaps, in every way except for the purpose of printing them for profit. You are not to buy my lectures to sell again. You come here to hear them for your own use, and for your own use you may take notes." In the case of Lord Clarendon's work,[1] the history was lent to a person, and an application was made for an injunction to stay the publication. It was said there that there was no ground for an injunction, and it was proved on affidavit that my Lord Clarendon's son said, "There is the book, make what use you please of it." The Chancellor, however, of that day, said that he could not mean he was to print it for his profit. So with respect to letters, my Lord Hardwicke

---

[1] *Duke of Queensberry* v. *Shebbeare*, 2 Eden, 329.

says in one case[1] that the person who parts with letters still retains a species of property in them, and that the person who receives them has also a species of property in them. He may do what he pleases with the papers. He may make what use he pleases of the letters except print them.'

Since September 1835, authors of lectures have had the protection of Statute Law, 5 & 6 William IV. c. 65 (entitled, 'An Act for Preventing the Publication of Lectures without consent'), giving to the author of any lectures or his assignee (subject to certain formalities and restrictions) the right to prevent the publication of such lectures, and prescribing penalties for infringement of his right.

After stating 'that printers, publishers, and other persons, have frequently taken the liberty of printing and publishing lectures delivered upon divers subjects, without the consent of the authors of such lectures,' sec. 1 enacts 'that from and after the 1st day of September, 1835, the author of any lecture or lectures, or the person to whom he hath sold or otherwise conveyed the copy thereof, in order to *deliver* the same . . . shall have the sole right and liberty of printing and publishing such lecture or lectures.' Printing and publishing without leave of the author or his assignee is punishable by forfeiture of the spurious copies, and of a penalty of one penny a sheet for all found in the offender's custody, one moiety of the penalty going to the Crown, and the other to the party suing for it.

The third section of the Act declares 'that no person allowed for certain fee and reward or otherwise to attend and be present at any lecture delivered in any place shall be deemed and taken to be licensed or to have leave to print, copy and publish such lectures, only because of having leave to attend such lecture or lectures.'

The Act requires (§ 5) that notice in writing of the printing, copying, or publishing any lecture which is to

[1] *Pope* v. *Curl*, 2 Atk. 342.

be protected by the Act be given to two justices living within five miles from the place where such lecture or lectures shall be delivered two days at the least before delivering the same. The Act does not apply 'to any lecture or lectures delivered in any university, or public school, or college, or on any public foundation, or by any individual in virtue of, or according to, any gift, endowment, or foundation.'

The Act prohibits the printing, copying, publishing, and exposing for sale. It says nothing about the *delivery* of lectures. What would the decision of the Court be in a case similar to *Abernethy* v. *Hutchinson* if, instead of printing and publishing lectures, the editor of a newspaper, or any other person, were to deliver them as taken down? Would such an Act come within the definition of 'copying'? It seems singular that the point should have escaped attention, unless the reservation to the author of his right at Common Law is supposed to cover the omission.

I am not aware of any case in which so called 'Dramatic Readings" (which would come within the same principle as lectures) have been objected to by dramatic authors. Charles Dickens's works have been constantly so read.[1]

III. NATURE OF STAGERIGHT.

The next point we have to consider is the subject matter out of which the right we are concerned with arises. It is one in which little difficulty will be experienced, the doubts formerly entertained in *Bach* v. *Longman*[2] and similar cases, having been obviated by the large wording of the statutes which protect the right. By 3 & 4 Will. IV. c. 15, this subject matter is declared to be 'any tragedy, comedy, play, opera, farce, and any other dramatic

---

[1] See per Wood, V.C., *Tinsley* v. *Lacy*, 1863, 1 H. and M. 747.
[2] 1777 (Bach's Sonata), Cowp. 623.; *Pope* v. *Curl*, 1741, cited 4 Burr. 2330.

piece or entertainment'; and by 5 & 6 Vic. c. 45, the words 'dramatic piece' are declared to include 'every tragedy, comedy, play, opera, farce, or other scenic, musical, or dramatic entertainment.'

The Act would seem to extend only to restrain representation in 'places of dramatic entertainment,' but the Courts have construed it in conformity with the object the legislature is supposed to have had in view in framing it, and have decided that the admission of spectators on payment[1] to any place in which the representation is conducted constitutes that place a 'place of dramatic entertainment within the meaning of the Act.' In the course of the argument in the famous case of *Russell* v. *Smith*,[2] Patteson, J., observed upon the plaintiff's contention, and apparently without dissenting from it:—' The plaintiff contends that the place is so if the performance is dramatic. He would say that the street where Punch is performed is for the time being a place of dramatic entertainment.' In that case the defendant sung at Crosby Hall, a place licensed for music and dancing under Geo. II. c. 36, a song of the plaintiff's called, ' The Ship on Fire,' and the question was whether under secs. 20, 21, & 24 of 5 & 6 Vic. c. 45, taken in connection with secs. 1 & 2 of 3 & 4 Will. IV. c. 15, such a composition was protected. The nature of the song was such that it was not necessary to determine the whole question raised, the judgment of the Court being to the effect that assuming dramatic character to be necessary to a song to entitle it to protection, a song which relates the burning of a ship at sea, and the escape of those on board, describes their feelings in vehement language, and sometimes expresses them in the supposed words of the suffering parties, is dramatic, and therefore within the statute, although sung by only one person sitting at a piano, unassisted by scenery;

[1] See as to the infringement of copyright by gratuitous distribution of copies, *Novello* v. *Sudlow*, 12 C.B. 177.
[2] 12 Q.B. 233.

and further that the room in which the song is performed, and to which persons paying for tickets are admitted for the purpose of hearing it, is for the time a place of dramatic entertainment, though that room be ordinarily used for different purposes. The use for the time is the essential fact. 'As a regular theatre may be lecture-room, dining-room, ball-room, and concert-room, on successive days, so a room used ordinarily for either of those purposes would become, for the time being, a theatre if used for the representation of a regular stage play.'

This decision was followed in *Russell* v. *Briant*[1] where the 'Horns Tavern' was the place of entertainment.

Whether there has been representation is a question of fact, representing being the 'bringing forward on a stage or place of public entertainment.' If the words of one song only of a musical or dramatic piece [2] protected by the Act be so brought forward without the permission of the proprietor of the stageright the representation will be actionable.[3]

As regards the place of representation therefore we may infer from the above cases, proprietors of stageright are likely to meet with few difficulties under the Act; while, so far as the subject-matter of their compositions is concerned, the wording of the several Acts is also, as has been already observed, highly favourable to dramatic and musical authors. Their compositions while in MS. and in print[4] come of course within the law applicable to other literary compositions as regards copyright.

[1] 19 L.J. C.P. 33. The word 'copyright' is used in this case by Wilde C.J., to denote the right infringed by the defendant in singing plaintiff's songs 'The Ship on Fire,' and 'The Gambler's Wife.'

[2] *Planché* v. *Braham*, 1837, 'The Enchanted Horn,' 8 C. and P. 68, 1 Jur. 823.

[3] See *Lee* v. *Simpson*, 3 C.B. 2871.

[4] As to the property of an author in an unpublished work independently of the statute of Anne see *Duke of Queensbury* v. *Shebbeare*, 2 Eden, 329, *Southey* v. *Sherwood*, 2 Mer. 436, *Thompson* v. *Stanhope*, Amb. 737.

A sheet of music comes within the definition of a 'book,' by 5 & 6 Vic. c. 45, § 2.

It is worth noting here, as conflicting with modern decisions in respect of an important principle, that Lord Mansfield, in the very case [1] which established the right of the musical composer to the protection of the statute of Anne so far as the publication of his work was concerned, expressed himself as of opinion that he could have no claim to restrain the performance of his composition. 'A person,' his lordship said, 'may use the copy by playing it,[2] but he has no right to rob the author of the profit by multiplying copies and disposing of them to his own use.'

It is easy, of course, to see that there must be a line beyond which the modern doctrine would not extend. That doctrine, in its strictness, would prevent the performance for profit of a song without recognition of the owner's right to remuneration; and, as a matter of principle, no doubt, the author may be said to be entitled to the entire profit arising from his production. The question of how far he is entitled by Law to this profit was much discussed in early cases, and occasionally assumed a somewhat curious form. In *Tonson* v. *Collins*[3] Counsel Thurlow asks, 'Does an action lie against the keepers of circulating libraries who buy one book and lend it to a hundred to read?' To which Blackstone replies, 'Certainly not. The purchaser of a single book may make any use he pleases of it, but no man has the right of making new books by multiplying copies of the old. If a man has an opera ticket he may lend it to as many friends as he pleases, but he may not counterfeit the impression and forge others. The owner of a single guinea may barter it, or lend it, but he may not copy the die and coin another.'

[1] *Bach* v. *Longman*, 1777, Cowp. 623; *Russell* v. *Smith*, 12 Q.B. 217.
[2] See as to the present law *Planché* v. *Braham*, 8 C. and P. 68.
[3] 1762, 1 W. Bl. 325.

That the rights of an author are unaffected by the fact of his manuscript being, with his consent, and for other than valuable consideration, in their hands, we may take to have been established Law, since Lord Hardwicke, in *Pope* v. *Curl*,[1] granting an injunction as to Pope's letters to Swift, thought 'sending a letter transferred the paper upon which it was wrote and every use of the contents except the liberty and profit of publishing.' Practically, so far as the right of performance of music is concerned, the line is marked out by the composer's interest, as represented by his copyright, the performance of a song by a popular singer creating a demand for the song in print.

An arrangement for the pianoforte of the score of an opera was held in *Wood* v. *Boosey*, 7 B. and S. 869, to be an independent work, although, if published during the existence of Copyright in the original opera, it would have been an infringement of Copyright therein. An introduction to a pantomime, which is the only written part of such an entertainment, is within the protection of 5 & 6 Vic. c. 45. *Lee* v. *Simpson*, 1847, 3 C.B. 871.

The refusal by the Courts to protect an author in his stageright by reason of his composition offending public morality is hardly likely to occur with reference to the London stage, but the occurrence recently of a case[2] in which the Lord Chamberlain[3] interposed to prevent certain high personages being represented in ludicrous positions upon the stage, suggests the possibility of caricature upon the stage analogous to libel in a literary work.[4] In *Walcot* v. *Walker*,[5] a case depending on agreement, Lord Eldon, after referring to an opinion of Eyre C.J., not reported, said that ' if the doctrine of the Chief Justice was right,

---

[1] 1741. 2 Atk. 342. See *Abernethy* v. *Hutchinson*, 3 L.J. Ch. 209, where the judgment is cited with approval by Lord Eldon.

[2] The 'Happy Land' at the Court Theatre.

[3] The Lord Chamberlain's Act, 6 and 7 Vic. c. 68, is given in the Appendix.

[4] Note D, Appendix, 'Caricature.'

[5] 7 Ves. 1.

and he had no doubt it was, that publications might be of such a nature that the author could maintain no action at law, it was not the business of that Court, even upon the submission in the answer, to decree either an injunction or an account of the profits of works of such a nature that the author can maintain no action at Law for the imitation of that which he calls his property.'

In *Hime* v. *Dale*,[1] which was an action for printing the words of a song called 'Abraham Newland,' Lord Ellenborough was inclined to think that such a publication was not protected by 8 Anne c. 19, but only because the word 'book' did not apply to a single sheet.

Garrow, in the course of the argument, drew their lordships' attention to the libellous nature of the song, and contended that it was of such a description that it could not receive the protection of the law in whatever shape it had appeared. It professed to be a panegyric upon money, but was in reality a gross libel upon the administration of justice. The object of the composition was to excite the people against the ministers of the law and the duties they had to perform. The mischievous tendency of the production was argued from the following stanza :—

> The world is inclined
> To think Justice blind,
> Yet what of all that?
> She will blink like a bat
> At the sight of friend Abraham Newland.
> Oh Abraham Newland! Magical Abraham Newland!
> Tho' Justice 'tis known,
> Can see thro' a mill-stone,
> She can't see through Abraham Newland.

Lord Ellenborough.—If the composition appeared on the face of it to be a libel so gross as to affect the public morals, I should advise the jury to give no damages. I know the Court of Chancery on such an occasion would grant no injunction.

[1] 1803, cited in a note to *Clementi* v. *Golding*, 2 Camp. N.P. 27. As to the jurisdiction of the Court in cases of this character, see a note by Sweet in Jarman & Bythewood, Preced. 3 ed. vol. vii. 637.

Lawrence, J.—The argument used by Mr. Garrow on this fugitive piece as being a libel would as forcibly apply to the 'Beggars' Opera,' where the language and allusions are sufficiently derogatory to the administration of public justice.

As regards the nature of the right in respect of devolution little need be said. The connexion in its origin of copyright with patentright, and of the latter with various franchises which in early times were of a doubtful kind,[1] induced possibly the introduction into the Copyright Amendment Act of a declaration[2] that 'all copyright' (and stageright presumably as well) 'shall be deemed personal property, and shall be transmissible by bequest, or in cases of intestacy[3] shall be subject to the same law of distribution as other personal property, and in Scotland shall be deemed to be personal and moveable estate.'

It being contended in *Marsh* v. *Conquest*[4] that, notwithstanding the statute 5 & 6 Vic. c. 45, Stageright was not assignable, Erle, C. J., observed: 'It is true that the sole right of representation did not exist at Common Law, *Murray* v. *Elliston* 5 B. and Ald. 657. 1 D. and R. 299. But the statute having made that a property, is it not subject to all the incidents of property, one of which is that it shall be assignable? Unless there be anything in the statute to prohibit it, I am prepared to hold that the power to assign the right of representation does exist.'

'The personal nature of Copyright,' observes Mr. Sweet

---

[1] It seems at one time to have been questioned whether a *caronne* or licence by the Mayor of London to keep a cart was a chattel interest and belonged to the executor, or whether it passed to the heir. Com. Dig. "Biens" B *Hunt* v. *Hunt*, 2 Vern. 83.

[2] 5 and 6 Vic. c. 45 § 25.

[3] See as to Bankruptcy *Re Baldwin* 1858, 2 De G. & J. 230; *Longman* v. *Tripp* 1805, 2 Bos. and P. (N.S.) 67.

[4] 1864, 17 C.B. (N.S.) 426. This passage is interesting as indicating his Lordship's opinion that if *Murray* v. *Elliston* were over-ruled, stageright might exist at Common Law.

in his notes to Jarman & Bythewood (Preced. 3 ed. vol. vii. 617) 'though never before made a subject of direct enactment, has always been assumed, see *Duke of Queensbury* v. *Shebbeare*. Some Scotch lawyers have unaccountably fallen into the mistake of treating Patentright and Copyright as heritable property. See Bell's Commentaries, I. 115.'

Lecture-right, under the statute, would, I apprehend, be subject to almost precisely the same limitations in this respect as stageright and copyright.

We may remark before concluding this branch of the subject, that in *Fitzball* v. *Brooke*,[1] it was held that the defendant, who had been arrested in execution in an action for penalties, was entitled to be discharged under the 7 & 8 Vic. c. 96, § 57; the action being one 'for the recovery of a *debt*,' within the meaning of that statute.[2]

As regards Titles of plays, the subject comes so close to that of trademarks, that the same considerations which have been applied in reference to cases connected with the titles of newspapers, books, and articles of trade,[3] would doubtless guide the Court in its decision. So far back as *Tonson* v. *Collins*,[4] Lord Mansfield observed, 'There are many decrees which make these things assets. I remember one with regard to the title of the *St. James's Evening Post*. The buyer was quieted in the possession of it, and no one else permitted to set it up.'

From what has been said it is clear that stageright (or 'stage copyright' as Mr. Justice Erle has called it), although

---

[1] 1845, 2 D. and L. 477.

[2] See as to the conditions under which the discharge of a bankrupt is now granted. The Bankruptcy Acts of 1869, § 48.

[3] *Clement* v. *Maddick*, ('Bell's Life in London,' and 'Sporting Chronicle') ('The Penny Bell's Life,' and 'Sporting News,') 5 Jur. (N.S.) 592. *Seixo* v. *Provezende*, ('Seixo with a crown' to denote a quality of wine,) ('Crown Seixo de Cima,') L.R. 1 Ch. Appendix, 192; *Maxwell* v. *Hogg*, *Hogg* v. *Maxwell*, ('Belgravia Magazine,') L.R. 2 Ch. Appendix, 307.

[4] 1762, 1 W. Bl. 335.

it has never found a separate name, is in its essence entirely independent of copyright. The precise language in which this is declared in Sec. 22 of 5 & 6 Vic. c. 45 is said to be due to the decision in *Cumberland* v. *Planché*,[1] decided in 1834, when the Court seems to have held that stageright was ancillary to, not co-ordinate with, copyright.

The section referred to enacts that no assignment of the copyright of any book consisting of or containing a dramatic piece or musical composition shall be holden to convey to the assignee the right of representing or performing such dramatic piece or musical composition, unless an entry in the registry book at Stationers' Hall shall be made of such assignment, 'wherein shall be expressed the intention of the parties that such right should pass by such assignment.' See *Marsh* v. *Conquest*, 17 C.B. N.S. 418.

3 & 4 Will. c. 15 prohibits (§ 2) the representation or performance of matter protected by the Act 'without the consent in writing of the author or other proprietor first had and obtained,' and the onus of proving this consent in an action for penalties lies on the defendant.

The consent may be prospective. The plaintiff in a case[2] in which the point was fully discussed was a member of a society called The Dramatic Authors' Society. The society issued lists of the several dramas composed by its members, with the prices charged for each night's performance if represented with the consent of the Society, such permission to be granted conditionally on the party representing the piece furnishing a monthly file of bills and payment within a given time of the account rendered. The latest of these lists was published in 1846. In 1849 the secretary gave the defendant a written permission in these terms: 'Mr. C. has permission to play dramas belonging to the authors forming the Dramatic

---

[1] 'The Greeneyed Monster,' 1 Ad. and E. 58, 3 N. and M. 537.
[2] *Morton* v. *Copeland*, 1855, 16 C.B. 517.

Authors' Society, upon his punctual transmission of monthly bills and payment of the prices for the performances of such dramas.' The plaintiff sued the defendant for penalties for representing the dramas composed by him since the year 1849. Held that the licence so given by the secretary (the authorised agent of the plaintiff for that purpose), coupled with the original list and prospectus, applied to the dramas composed by members of the Society after the date of the licence as well as to those composed before.

The statute simply requires that the consent shall be the act of the proprietor, and shall be in writing. 'The necessity for signature,' Mr. Justice Maule observed in the case now cited, 'arises in every case from the express requirement of the statute. Signature does not necessarily mean writing a person's Christian and surname, but any mark which identifies it as the act of the party.'

As to the territorial extent of the right, 5 & 6 Vic. c. 45 enacts (§ 2) ' that the words " British dominions" in that Act shall be construed to mean and include all parts of the United Kingdom of Great Britain and Ireland, the islands of Jersey and Guernsey, all parts of the East and West Indies, and all the colonies,[1] settlements, and possessions of the Crown which now are or hereafter may be acquired.'

IV. PROPRIETOR OF STAGE-RIGHT.

We have seen in respect of what matter stage-right arises. We have now to consider who is, in law, the proprietor of that right, and what steps are necessary to vest it in an assignee. The original proprietor, one would naturally be inclined to think, must be the author or composer of the matter performed. Here, however, the

---

[1] *Low* v. *Routledge*, 35 L.J. 114 Ch.; 13 L.T. (N.S.) 421.

special circumstances of the case necessitate in practice some deviations from strict principle. In cases in which the composer is the paid agent of the manager, and the composition accessory only to the general arrangement of the play, the author has been held to have composed for the benefit of the manager, and the stageright as to the accessory to be in the person who has arranged the entire play.

The principle on which this class of cases rests was laid down with great clearness by Erle, C.J., in *Hatton* v. *Kean*.[1] In that case Mr. Kean had organized a grand Shakesperian revival, and employed the plaintiff to compose a piece of music as part of the spectacle. 'I am of opinion,' his Lordship said, 'that the music so composed by the direction and under the superintendence of the defendant, and as part of the general plan of the spectacle, must, as between him and the plaintiff, become the property of the defendant, and that consequently the defendant has violated no right of the plaintiff in causing it to be represented in the manner alleged. One cannot but perceive that if the plaintiff were right in his contention the labour and skill and capital bestowed by the defendant upon the preparation of the entertainment might all be thrown away, and the entire object of it frustrated, and the speculation defeated by any one contributor withdrawing his portion. As between these parties and under these circumstances it seems to me very clearly that the musical composition in question became the property of the defendant, and that the plaintiff never was, within the language of the statute, the owner or proprietor thereof.'

Mr. Justice Willes, in concurring in the judgment, said, 'All I desire to add is that in coming to this conclusion we decide nothing that is inconsistent with the decision of this Court in *Shepherd* v. *Conquest*, 17 C.B. 427,

---

[1] 1859, 17 C.B. (N.S.) 268; 29 L.J. C.P. 20; and L.T. (N.S.) 10.

inasmuch as this case falls within the class, as to which the Court there expressly disclaimed giving any opinion.'

The case of *Shepherd* v. *Conquest*[1] referred to by his lordship was this. The proprietors of a theatre employed an author to compose for them a dramatic piece, paying him a weekly salary and travelling expenses. There was no contract in writing, nor any assignment or registry of the copyright, but a mere verbal understanding that the plaintiffs were to have the sole right of representing the piece in London. It was held that the plaintiffs were not the assignees of the copyright, nor had they such a right or interest therein as to entitle them to maintain an action for penalties under the 3 & 4 Will. IV., c. 15, § 2. The decision left it a matter of doubt—1. Whether, under any circumstances, the copyright in a literary work, or the sole right of representation, can become vested *ab initio* in an employer other than the person who has actually composed or adapted a literary work; and 2. Whether there can be a partial assignment of a copyright.

The judgment of the Court was thus delivered by Jervis, C.J. :—' This is an action for an alleged piracy of a dramatic piece called " Old Joe and Young Joe," the exclusive right of representing which upon the London stage is alleged to belong to the plaintiffs. It appears that the plaintiffs, being the proprietors of the Surrey Theatre, agreed by word of mouth with one Courtney that the latter should go to Paris for the purpose of adapting a piece there in vogue for representation upon the English stage, that the plaintiffs should pay all Courtney's expenses, and should have the sole right of representing the piece in London, Courtney retaining the right of representation in the provinces. Courtney accordingly proceeded to Paris, produced the piece in question, and was paid by the plaintiffs as agreed. The piece

---

[1] 1856, 17 C.B. 427 ; 2 Jur. (N.S.) 236 ; 25 L.J. C.P. 127.

was brought out at the Surrey Theatre by the plaintiffs, and afterwards at the Grecian Saloon by the defendant, who had obtained an assignment from Courtney. The question is whether the plaintiffs, by the transaction between them and Courtney, became entitled to the sole right of representation of the piece in London, so as to be able to maintain the action.' His lordship, after citing 3 & 4 Will. IV. c. 15, §§ 1 & 2, continued:—' It could not be successfully contended for the plaintiffs that a right once acquired under this statute could be assigned without writing. The 2nd section, in rendering a consent in writing necessary to justify a single representation, involves the consequence that an assignment conveying the exclusive right to represent throughout her Majesty's dominions, or (if that be possible) in some definite part of them, must, in order to be valid, be in writing, and there was no such assignment to the plaintiffs. They have no right, therefore, unless it can be established that by reason of the relation between them and Courtney the right vested in them at the moment when the piece was composed. Accordingly, it was contended on their behalf that, under the circumstances, Courtney was to be considered as merely their servant, the produce of whose labour became the property of his masters at the moment of production, so that no assignment was necessary to vest that property in the latter; and the case was likened to those relating to patent inventions, in which suggestions of servants employed in perfecting a discovery tending to facilitate its practical application may be adopted by the employer, and incorporated into his main design, without detracting from the originality necessary to sustain a patent for the entire scheme. To those might be added *Barfield* v. *Nicholson* (2 Sim. & S. 1), in which Sir J. Leach suggested the application of a similar principle to copyright, in the following words: " I am of opinion that under that statute (8 Anne c. 19) the person who forms the plan and who embarks in the speculation of a work and who employs various persons to compose different parts of it, adapted to their own peculiar acquirements—that he, the person who so forms the plan and scheme of the work, and pays different artists of his own selection, who upon certain conditions contribute to it, is the author and proprietor of the work, if not within the literal expression, at least within equitable meaning of the Statute of Anne, which being a remedial law, is to be construed liberally." Also it may be added, that in the extract from Merlin, *Repertoire de Jurisprudence*, tit. "*Contrefaçon*" S. 11, the words "author" and "inventor" are said to be synonymous; and, indeed, it has been contended that the productions of an author are to be dealt with in the same manner as the inventions of a workman, and that the former, like the latter, may become the property of an employer who hires the author's labours, and as it were buys his brains. To this it was answered, that literary productions stand upon different and higher ground from that occupied by mechanical inventions: that the intention of the legislature in the enactments relating to copyright was to elevate and protect literary men; that such an intention could only be effectuated by holding that the actual composer of the work was the author and proprietor of the copyright; and that no relation existing between him and an employer who himself took no intellectual part in the production of the work could without an assignment in writing vest the proprietorship of it in the latter. To this might be added, as to literary property and patents for inventions, that they are both creatures of statutes; that the enactments on which they are respectively founded differ widely in their origin and in their details; and that in order to shew that the position and rights of an author within the Copyright Acts are not to be measured by those of an inventor within the patent laws, it is only necessary to bear in mind that whilst, on the one hand, a person imports from abroad the invention of another, previously unknown here, without any further originality or merit in himself, is an inventor entitled to a patent; on the other hand, a person who merely reprints for the first time in this country a valuable foreign work, without bestowing upon it any intellectual labour of his own, as by translation (which to some extent must impress a new character), cannot thereby acquire the title of an author within the statutes relating to copyright. We do not think it necessary in the present case to express an opinion whether under any circumstances the copyright in a literary work, or the right of representation in a dramatic one, can become vested *ab initio* in an employer other than the person who has actually composed or adapted the work. It is enough to say in the present case, that no such effect can be produced where the employers merely suggest the subject and have no share in the design or execution of the work, the whole of which, so far as any character of originality belongs to it, flows from the mind of the person employed. It appears to us an abuse of terms to say that in such a case the employers are the authors of a work to which their minds have not contributed an idea; and it is upon the author in the first instance that the right is conferred by the statute which creates it. We cannot bring our minds to any other conclusion than that Courtney, the person who actually made the adaptation, though at the suggestion of the plaintiffs, acquired for himself as author of the adaptation, and so far as that adaptation gave any new character to the work, the statutory right of representing it; and that inasmuch as the plaintiffs have no assignment in writing of that right, they cannot sue for any infringement of it. As to the case of *Sweet* v. *Benning*, referred to as an authority in favour of the plaintiffs, the decision there turned upon the construction of the peculiar provisions of the 18th sec. of the 5 & 6 Vict. c. 45, relating to periodical works, and it has no bearing upon the present case.'

In *Wallerstein* v. *Herbert* [1] the plaintiff was engaged by A. B. at the St. James' Theatre as musical director. Under his engagement he was, *inter alia*, to provide the music incidental to the dramatic performances, being either his original compositions, or selected from the works of other composers. A. B. being about to bring out at the theatre a drama called 'Lady Audley's Secret,' the plaintiff composed the music for it, and it was brought out accordingly, the music being merely accessory to the drama for the purpose of increasing the effect of certain situations. A. B. having discontinued the management of the theatre, was succeeded by the defendant, to whom he handed over the drama, together with the music, and which the defendant subsequently performed without the consent of the plaintiff. It was here held in an action for penalties (confirming the decision of *Hatton* v. *Kean* [2]) that, under the circumstances, the plaintiff had no stage-right in the music.

'Looking at the nature of the composition,' said Cockburn, C.J., 'it is clear that it became part and parcel of the drama, and was not an independent composition.'

Shee, J., observed that it was incumbent on the plaintiff to show that he retained an independent right to the music.

The same principle has been recognised by the American Courts. In *Keene* v. *Wheatley*,[3] 9 Amer. L. R. 47, the plaintiff was employed as general assistant of the defendant in the representation of a play, and it was held that the latter was the proprietor of the right, on the principle that where an inventor, in the course of his experimental essays, employs an assistant, who suggests and adapts a subordinate improvement, it is in law an incident or part of the employer's main invention.

The point is a very old one. In *Storace* v. *Longman*,[4] a case in the last century, we find the defendant contending

---

[1] 1867, 16 L.T. (N.S.) 453; 15 W.R. 838.
[2] *Ante*, p. 59.   [3] Cited in *Palmer v. Dewitt*.
[4] 1788. Cited in a note to *Clementi v. Golding*, 2 Camp. 27.

that the song pirated (by printing) was composed to be sung by the plaintiff's sister at the Italian Opera, and that all compositions so performed were the property of the *house*, not of the composer. Lord Kenyon said that this defence could not be supported; that the statute vested the property in the author; and that no such private regulation could interfere with the public right.

A frequent practice in former days, and one which is not unknown at the present day, is that of joint authorship. We have a familiar instance of such 'collaboration' for the stage in the plays of Beaumont and Fletcher, and judging from the entries in Henslowe's Diary, one would feel inclined to say that the composition of a play by a single hand for the theatres under his management was rather the exception than the rule. Sometimes as many as six authors seem to have been engaged at once, by this thriftiest of managers, on a single play.

A very recent case, *Levi* v. *Rutley*,[1] shows that the employment of an author to write a play, and even the suggestion by the employer of the subject, does not thereby constitute the employer proprietor of the copyright in the play; and the further doctrine was laid down in that case, that to constitute a joint authorship of a dramatic piece or other literary work it must be the result of a preconcerted joint design. Mere alterations, additions, or improvements by another person, whether with or without the sanction of the author, will not entitle such other person to be considered the 'joint author' of the work.

The facts of the case were these: The plaintiff, the lessee of a theatre, employed one W. to write a play for him, and suggested the subject. W. having completed it, the plaintiff and some members of his company introduced various alterations in the incidents and in the dialogue to make the play more attractive; and one of them wrote an additional scene. It was held that the plaintiff was not the joint author of the play with W.

[1] 1871, L.R. 6, C.P. 523.

The play being finished, a sum of 4*l*. 15*s*. was paid to W. on account, and he signed a receipt drawn up by the plaintiff's attorney as follows:—' Received of Mr. L. (the plaintiff) the sum of 4*l*. 15*s*. [on] account of 15 guineas, for my share, title, and interest as co-author with him in the drama intituled "The King's Wager;" balance of 15 guineas to be paid on assigning my share to him.' The balance was never paid, nor was any assignment executed by W. These facts were held to be no evidence that the plaintiff was either 'joint author' or assignee of the author.

Agreements to write for the stage, like agreements to act,[1] are, of course, not enforceable. The only remedy is by an action for breach of contract. In *Morris* v. *Colman*,[2] Colman, who was a partner with plaintiff and others in the Haymarket Theatre, entered into an agreement not that he would write for the Haymarket, but that he would not write for any other theatre, and an injunction was granted restraining him.

As might be expected from what has been already said as to the legal *status* of a foreign author according to English law, considerable difficulties are introduced into the subject of copyright and stageright where the author is a foreigner resident abroad at the time when his work is first published in England.

As a review of the Law on this subject *Jeffreys* v. *Boosey*[3] will well repay attention, the judgment of the House of Lords in that case having reversed the unanimous judgment of the Exchequer Chamber, by which, in turn, the judgment of the Court of Exchequer had been reversed. The facts were these: Bellini, a foreigner resident at Milan, composed a musical work, of which he assigned the copyright to R., according to Milanese law. R. was also a foreigner. R. came to London and assigned

---

[1] As to the course pursued with reference to an actor under these circumstances, see *Webster* v. *Dillon*, 3 Jur. (N.S.) 432; 5 W.R. 867; and as to a singer similarly restrained, *Lumley* v. *Wagner*, 5 De G. & S. 485; 1 De G. M. & G. 604.

[2] 18 Ves. 437.   [3] 1855, 4 H. of L. Ca. 866; 1 Jur. (N.S.) 615.

his interest to Boosey, an Englishman, 'but for publication in Great Britain and Ireland only,' and thereupon the first publication took place in England. It was held by the House of Lords, upon these facts, that Boosey had no copyright in the work. The statute of Anne, it was said, was not intended to apply to foreign authors. But where a foreign author owed a temporary allegiance to the Crown by residence in England at the time of the first publication of his work—the work not having been previously published elsewhere—he was an author within the meaning of the statute.

It was the opinion of Lord St. Leonards that, assuming Bellini had a right to copyright in England, he ought, in order to entitle the assignee, to have assigned it according to the law of England. His Lordship laid down another most important principle, viz. that the assignment from R. to Boosey being confined to copyright in Great Britain and Ireland was bad, for ' there cannot be a partial assignment of copyright '—a *dictum* directly conflicting with the opinion of some very eminent judges, and notably with that of Erle, C. J. Lord St. Leonards' views were thus expressed:[1] ' The simple question is, as has been truly stated, whether a foreigner can obtain an English copyright by publishing here although he be resident abroad. Now that right has been claimed on two grounds : First, upon a supposed or asserted Common Law right, to which reference has already been made. My lords, upon the Common Law right I have never, at least for many years, been able to entertain any doubt. It is a question which I have often in my professional life had occasion to consider, and upon which I have arrived long since at the conclusion that no such right exists after publication. I never could in my own mind distinguish between the right to an invention after publication, and the right to the description of that invention after the publication of that description.'

' The question whether a foreigner publishing in England can sue in this country for his copyright was,' said

[1] 1 Jur. (N.S.) 648.

Lord Lyndhurst, in *D'Almaine* v. *Boosey*,[1] 'determined in the case of *Bach* v. *Longman* (Cowp. 623). Bach was a musical composer, who had come into this country from Germany. He sued Longman for pirating a sonata, which the latter had published in England, and was successful in his suit. The argument, however, in that case turned chiefly on a question which may properly be considered here, viz. whether music is within the statute of Anne. From the expressions of Lord Mansfield, it is clear that he considered printed music to be nothing more than a shorthand mode of representing what might be written in another manner at great length. In *Hime* v. *Dale* (2 Camp. 27*n*) this doctrine was doubted. I was for the plaintiff in that action, which was brought for an infraction of copyright, and I remember that Lord Ellenborough doubted not only whether music was within the provisions of the statutes, but also whether music printed on a single sheet was a book. Having to investigate the subject for the purpose of moving for a new trial, I spent three or four days at Stationers' Hall in order to ascertain what entries were made under the Act of Parliament, and I found not only that short publications on single sheets of paper were entered as books, but also a great deal of music. There is no doubt, therefore, that printed music, in whatever form it is published, is to be considered, in reference to proceedings of this nature, as a book.'

The subject of alien authors generally was much discussed in this case, in which it was decided that the English assignee of a foreign author was within the protection of the Copyright Act, and a strong opinion was expressed that a foreigner who resided in England and published here enjoyed similar protection.

In *Clementi* v. *Walker*,[2] a foreign author, having published a song ('Vive Henri Quatre!') abroad in 1814, agreed to sell A the exclusive right to print it in this country. The agreement was not in writing. In September 1814 A

---

[1] 1835, 1 Y. & C. Ex. Eq. 298 (dance music).
[2] 1824, 2 B. & Cr. 861.

published the song here. In 1818 B published it here. In 1822 the author assigned to A in writing the exclusive right of printing in England.[1] *Held*, 1st, that A did not, by the part consent of 1814, acquire the exclusive right of publishing in England; 2nd, that that could not be deemed a publication by an author which was not made on his account or for his benefit; and 3rd, that publication by B was lawful, and that the assignment of 1822 did not give A the right to sue B for selling a copy of the song subsequent to such assignment.

That an urgent need existed for the recognition either by statute or from the Bench of the rights of foreign authors long before the International Law existed, we may see from cases such as *Guichard* v. *Mori*.[2] There the defendant published a piece of music called 'The Charms of Berlin,' about a third of which consisted of a piece of music sold by the composer in 1820 to the plaintiff. The music had been published in France in 1814, six years before the sale to the plaintiff. 'The policy of our law,' observed Lyndhurst, C., 'recognises by statutes express in their wording that the importation of foreign inventions shall be encouraged in the same manner as the inventions made in this country and by natives. This is founded as well upon reason, sense, and justice, as it is upon policy. It appears that this piece of music was published in France by Kalkbrenner, or some one to whom he sold it so long ago as 1814, six years before the sale to the plaintiff. There can be no question then of the right of the defendant, or any one else, to publish it in this country.'

In *Cocks* v. *Purday*,[3] a case somewhat later, it was held that a foreigner resident abroad might acquire copyright in this country by publishing his work here, and that a contemporaneous publication abroad did not defeat such

---

[1] *Jeffreys* v. *Boosey*, per Lord St. Leonards, 1 Jur. (N.S.) 615.
[2] 1831, 9 L.J. Ch. 227.
[3] 1848, 5 C.B. 860: 'The Elfen Waltzes.'

right. By the law which prevailed in Austria, where A and B were domiciled, copyright was the property of the author, and assignment by word of mouth was good assignment. A assigned his right to B, and B before publication sold his copyright to C. It was held that the author's interest vested in C before publication, so as to make him an assignee within the meaning of 5 & 6 Vic. c. 45, § 3, and confer upon him a good derivative title.

Boucicault v. *Delafield* [1] was a case of stageright decided after the passing of the International Copyright Act. The plaintiff, a British subject, resident here, was the author of 'The Colleen Bawn,' a piece first performed in America (with which country there was no convention), but registered at Stationers' Hall on the day of its first representation in England. In a suit for an injunction to restrain the representation, James, V.C., said that he had no doubt that the representation was piratical, but that grave and serious difficulties arose as to the plaintiff's right, depending as it did upon the effect of 7 & 8 Vic. c. 12, § 19. 'This Act,' his Honor observed, 'enables her Majesty, by certain proceedings mentioned therein, to extend to those who first print or publish the various works therein mentioned abroad, or first represent dramatic performances abroad, the same rights and privileges as are acquired by those who do the same acts first in this country. It is admitted that Mr. Boucicault has not complied with any of the provisions of this Act; in truth he had no possibility of complying with them, no regulation having been made, as I believe, according to the course there pointed out, as to the international copyright between this country and America. The question then became a serious one,—whether or not, by this 19th clause, the privilege which was by former Acts conferred upon dramatic authors, and which Mr. Boucicault would undoubtedly possess, was annihilated. The argument against that view was that the former Acts were intended

[1] 9 Jur. (N.S.) 1282; 33 L.J. 38 Ch.; 12 W.R. 101.

to confer a right upon British subjects at all events, and that the object of that International Act was to extend to foreigners, under certain circumstances of reciprocity and otherwise, the advantages which British authors had in this country with regard to literary works and dramatic performances, and that it could not be contended that the true construction of the Act was to take away the privileges conferred upon British subjects. Nevertheless, I hold the general view of the clause to be one that cannot possibly be got over; therefore Mr. Boucicault's rights are virtually destroyed. Undoubtedly, too, the words are precise, and clearly exclude him. And as to the argument that it cannot be supposed that the Legislature intended to exclude British authors from the privileges already given to them by an Act which was intended to relieve principally authors of a foreign country, although, I may say, that this Act was intended, as all English Acts are, principally for the benefit of British subjects, yet, on the other hand, we must consider what the state of the law is. Now it was pressed very strongly in argument before me that, as the case of *Jeffreys* v. *Boosey* had not been determined when the 7 & 8 Vic. c. 12, was passed, it was therefore to be presumed that the law there laid down was not in the purview of the Legislature. It must, however, be presumed that the Legislature is cognisant of what the law is, and I therefore take the law to be as it is declared in *Jeffreys* v. *Boosey*. It is there laid down thus:—That a foreigner printing his work for the first time in England is entitled to the benefit of the copyright just as much as any British subject, if he is *bonâ fide* residing in England, and publishing his work here for the benefit of the English public; the conclusion of the House of Lords being that the Copyright Acts were intended to encourage this particular department of literature in this country, and only in this country. It was also determined in the same case that a foreigner (and I apprehend the case would be the same if he was an Englishman) first publishing his work abroad, would not come within the purview of those Acts; at all events, that a foreigner would not come within the purview of the original Copyright Act, and would not be entitled to the benefit of it. Now that being so, how would the law stand when this International Act was passed? If Mr. Boucicault had been an American, and had first represented his piece in this country, he would have been entitled to the provisions of the Dramatic Copyright Act. Then this Act is passed, extending to any nation with which the Queen may, through her Privy Council, enter into arrangements for that purpose pursuant to the Act, the privileges which are accorded to all people who first publish their works in this country. Now, this sort of double right is just the right which the 7 & 8 Vic. c. 12, intended to extinguish. It says that no one shall have this double right: he shall not have the right of performance in this country under one Act, and also have a right under this particular provision in the International Copyright Act. And, therefore, although it is not for me to comment upon the act of the Legislature, it seems possible that exact justice would be completely meted out if this excluding clause had been extended to all nations with whom such negotiations had been entered into. But that is not what is said. The 19th clause says, in effect, that this Act having been made, if any person, whether a British subject or not, chooses to deprive this country of the advantage of the first representation of his work, then he may get the right, if he thinks fit, under the arrangements which may have been come to with that country he so favours with his representation, pursuant to the 7 & 8 Vic. c. 12. If, however, he does not get it,—if he chooses to publish his performance in a country which has not entered into any treaty, or made any arrangement for that purpose, he may do so, but this country has nothing more to say to him, and he must be taken to have elected under which of the statutes which have been made respecting similar subjects he wishes to come, and by performing his work in one country instead of the other, he is thereby excluded from all advantage of publishing in the other. I cannot see anything to justify me in restraining the provision, or to say that it applies to foreigners, and does not apply to British subjects, because if I did so I shall be bound by parity of reasoning to say that any foreigner publishing first in this country, and acquiring a right under the existing law, would have to be deprived of that right by this Act, whilst a British subject would not be deprived of the benefit. The object of the Legislature seems to have been, in these cases, to secure in this country the benefit of the first publication, and to extend to any other country the same benefit only on certain conditions, namely, that reciprocity shall be afforded, and that the representation shall take place for the first time in England, which may be published afterwards in another country. I am bound to hold, therefore, that Mr. Boucicault's right fails.'

In *Wood* v. *Chart*[1] the Act of 1852 received further elucidation in another aspect of it at the hands of the same eminent judge. The intention of the framers of this Act, in providing for the deposit of an authorised translation, was to give English people the best opportunity possible of knowing the foreign work. The original work in this case was a French comedy called 'Frou-Frou.' The version sanctioned by the authors and published in England was entitled 'Like to Like.' The names of the characters and the scenes were altered from French to English, and in some instances English manners were substituted for French. There were considerable omissions and alterations of the dialogue. It was held that the version was not a translation within the meaning of the Act such as to entitle the foreign authors and their assignee to the benefit of the statute 15 Vic. c. 12, § 8, sub. 6. Such a translation must be a translation of the whole work. A version which the foreign author may sanction is not

[1] 1870, L.R. 10 Eq. 204; 22 L.T. (N.S.) 432; 39 L.J. 641 Ch.

sufficient. The proceeding on the author's part came, in the opinion of the Court, within the meaning of the words 'imitation or adaptation' in the Act. After observing that the plaintiff had 'gone out of his course to dig a pitfall for himself,' the learned judge said that the plaintiff 'might have obtained the full benefit of his assignment, and prevented any representation of the French play or any English translation of it, if he had employed a translator and said, "Now make a translation of this. Do not be thinking of adaptation or imitation for the English stage, but make a translation of it;" and if it had been published in this country, then it would have been quite open to the author, or the person claiming under the author, to have represented that translation with any abbreviation, with any excision, with any alteration, with any adaptation which he might have thought fit, for the purpose of making it more suitable to the English stage. I have no doubt whatever, if he had first published a translation, that he could then have acted the piece which Mr. Sutherland Edwards has called a "version," and that nobody else could have acted anything like that—anything approaching to that.'

So far as facilities for its transfer are concerned, stage-right, like copyright, enjoys very valuable privileges, the only formality needful for its assignment being entry in the Registry Book at Stationers' Hall. 5 and 6 Vic. c. 45, § 11, enacts 'that a Book of Registry, wherein may be registered the proprietorship in the copyright of books and assignments thereof, and in dramatic and musical pieces, whether in manuscript or otherwise, and licenses affecting such copyright, shall be kept at the Hall of the Stationers' Company;' and that a certified copy of the entry of such book shall be received in evidence in all summary proceedings, and shall be *primâ facie* proof of the right (§ 20) of representation or performance, but subject to be rebutted by other evidence.

By § 12 of the same Act, making a false entry or producing a false copy of the entry, is declared a misdemeanour. By § 13 the proprietor of copyright (and by the incorporation of this section with § 20, of stageright) may make entry[1] of the title of his book, the time of the first publication, the name and place of abode of the proprietor or part proprietor of the copyright[2] in the forms given in the Schedule to the Act, 'and that it shall be lawful for every such registered proprietor to assign his interest, *or any portion of his interest* therein, by making entry in the said Book of Registry of such assignment, and of the name and place of abode of the assignee, in the form given in that behalf in the said schedule,' on payment of a certain fee, 'and such assignment so entered shall be effectual in law to all intents and purposes whatsoever, without being subject to any stamp or duty, and shall be of the same force and effect as if such assignment had been made by deed.'[3]

[1] The entry at Stationers' Hall was before this Act compulsory, though habitually neglected by many publishers. Neglect to make the entry did not, however, affect the copyright.—*Beckford* v. *Hood*, 7 T.R. 620.

[2] The name of the author is not required to be stated, unless, of course, he is also the proprietor. The author of a book published anonymously and not registered at Stationers' Hall was, under the old law, entitled to protection.—*Beckford* v. *Hood*, 5 T.R. 620. Eldon, C , doubted whether the proprietor of a book brought out under a fictitious name was entitled to protection.—*Hogg* v. *Kirby*, 8 Vic. 215; (Sweet's note to *Jarman* v. *Bythewood*, vii. 611).

[3] 'The adoption of this mode of transfer is optional. The protection it affords from the assignee's bankruptcy, and its cheapness, will frequently recommend it; but as the Act does not provide for the entry of any special terms, if any such are made, the expense of an agreement stamp (or, if covenants are required, of a deed stamp) cannot be avoided. The Act affords the means, however, of escaping the *ad valorem* duty upon a sale in all cases. If the statutory form is adopted in case of a mortgage, the *ad valorem* stamp must be impressed on the instrument of defeasance. The statutory assignment is to have the force of an assignment by *deed*. Will it imply a covenant for quiet enjoyment? A deed was not requisite to an assignment under the old Acts, and the present Act does not require even the formality of a writing to an assignment *in pais*, as it may be called. But a license to print, or, in the language of the trade, an assignment of *an edition* of a work, is required to be in writing.'—§§ 15, 17. (Sweet's Notes.)

By § 14, parties aggrieved by entry in the Book of Registry may apply to a court of law in term time, or to a judge in vacation, who may order the entry to be varied or expunged.¹

By § 20, after reciting that it is expedient to extend the term of the sole liberty of representing dramatic pieces given by 3 & 4 Will. IV. c. 15, and 'to extend to musical compositions the benefit of that Act and also of this Act,' it is enacted that the provisions of that Act and ' of this Act shall apply to musical compositions, and that the sole liberty of representing or performing, or causing or permitting to be represented or performed, any dramatic piece or musical composition, shall enure and be the property of the author thereof and his assignees for the term in the Act provided for the copyright in books; and the provisions hereinbefore enacted in respect of the property in such copyright, and of registering the same, shall apply to the liberty of representing or performing any dramatic piece or musical composition as if the same were herein expressly re-enacted and applied thereto, save and except that the first public representation or performance of any dramatic piece or musical composition shall be deemed equivalent, in the construction of this Act, to the first publication of any book; provided always that in case of any dramatic piece or musical composition in manuscript, it shall be sufficient for the person having the sole liberty of representing or performing, or causing to be represented or performed, the same, to register only the title thereof, the name and place of abode of the author or composer thereof, the name and place of abode of the proprietor thereof, and the time and place of its first representation or performance.'

By § 24 of 5 & 6 Vic. c. 45, it is enacted 'that no proprietor of copyright in any book which shall be published after the passing of this Act shall maintain any

---

¹ *Ex parte* Davidson, 2 Jur. (N.S.) 1024.

action or suit at law or in equity, or any summary proceeding in respect of any infringement of such copyright, unless he shall, before commencing such action, suit, or proceeding have caused an entry to be made in the Book of Registry of the Stationers' Company of such book, pursuant to this Act; provided always that the omission to make such entry shall not affect the copyright in any book, but only the right to sue or proceed in respect of the infringement thereof as aforesaid; provided also that nothing herein contained shall prejudice the remedies which the proprietor of the sole liberty of representing any dramatic piece shall have' under 3 & 4 Will. IV. c. 15, ' or of this Act, although no entry shall be made in the Book of Registry aforesaid.'

The different modes in which copyright and stageright are treated in this section has given rise to much discussion, and established a difference between them as regards the necessity of registration. It was this distinction that enabled the plaintiff to succeed in *Clark* v. *Bishop*.[1] The plaintiff in that case was the proprietor, by assignment from the author, of a song which he sang in character. He had never registered or printed it. The defendant, without plaintiff's consent, printed and published in a penny book words closely resembling those of the song. In an action for infringement of the copyright of the song, it was held that the song was not a book, but a dramatic piece in a musical or dramatic entertainment within 5 & 6 Vic. c. 45, § 2, and did not therefore require registration under § 24. Martin, B., dissented.

As regards the necessity for registration in the case of stageright, Mellor, J., in *Lacy* v. *Rhys*[2], observed, with reference to the section just cited, ' It may be that the person who drew this Act, having in his mind the effect of the

---

[1] 1872, Ex. 25; L.T. 908.
[2] 1864, 4 B. & S. 873-883; 12 W.R. 309; 33 L.J. Q.B. 157; 10 Jur. (N.S.) 612.

former one (3 & 4 Will. IV. c. 15) and the decision of this Court in *Cumberland* v. *Planché*,[1] thought it necessary to expressly provide, by the 22nd section, that the effect of the assignment of the copyright should not be so extensive as that given to it by that decision, and therefore introduced the provision that it should not have that effect unless the intention of the parties was expressed in the Book of Registry. That may have been the object of the section. At all events, there is nothing in it, or any other, to require registration of an assignment of the acting right.'

In *Lacy* v. *Rhys*[1] the facts were as follows:—After the passing of 3 & 4 Will. IV. c. 15, the administrator of an author of a dramatic piece first acted in 1843, by deed, dated the 14th April, 1859, in consideration of 100*l.*, assigned to the plaintiff the copyright and stageright in all dramatic pieces written by the author. No entry of the assignment to the plaintiff had been made in the Registry Book in pursuance of statute 5 & 6 Vic. c. 45, § 22. The letters of administration were not stamped until March 1863. Held that the plaintiff might maintain an action for penalties under 3 & 4 Will. IV. c. 15, against the defendant for representing the piece without his license within twenty-eight years of its publication, the period for which the sole liberty of representation is given by that statute, although the deed was not registered under statute 5 & 6 Vic. c. 45, § 22. Quære per Cockburn, C. J.: Whether the plaintiff would be entitled to the benefit of 5 & 6 Vic. c. 45, without registration of the deed?

Per Cockburn, C. J.: 'While the enactment in § 24 of 5 & 6 Vic. c. 45, requires registration before a person can proceed to enforce any of the advantages which that Act gives, the second proviso leaves a person who would

[1] 1834, 1 Ad. & E. 580; 3 N. & M. 537. See *Shepherd* v. *Conquest*.
[2] 1864, 4 B. & S. 873–883; 12 W.R. 309; 33 L.J. Q.B. 157; 10 Jur. (N.S.) 612.

be entitled to proceed under statute 3 & 4 Will. IV. c. 15, in the same position as he was in before. There is nothing in the later statute which operates to prevent the plaintiff having the benefit of the provisions of the former statute, and therefore he may recover these penalties.'

The same decision was come to in the case of *Wood* v. *Boosey*,[1] where it was held that it is not necessary, under 5 & 6 Vic. 45, and 7 & 8 Vic. c. 12, that a person to whom copyright has been assigned, not according to the statutory form, but by an independent mode, should register the copyright in order to entitle him to bring an action for its infringement. In order to comply with 7 & 8 Vic. c. 12, § 6, the day and month of publication should be stated in the register. The year alone is not sufficient,[2] copyright dating from the day of publication. The full title of the work must be given. It is not necessary to mention the place of abode of the assignee.

In *Marsh* v. *Conquest*[3] it was held that it was competent to the assignee of stageright to sue for penalties under 3 & 4 Will. IV. c. 15, notwithstanding the assignment was not by deed or registered under 5 & 6 Vic. c. 45.

In *Cumberland* v. *Planché*[4] it was held that a person to whom the copyright of a dramatic piece had been assigned previously to and within ten years of the passing of 3 & 4 Will. IV. c. 15 was an assignee within that clause of the Act which gives to the author's assignee, in the case of a dramatic work published within ten years, the sole liberty of representing it. § 22 of 5 & 6 Vic. c. 45 does not apply where there is an assignment of the right of representing or performing. The assignee spoken of in the former Act is the assignee of the copyright of the dramatic piece, not of the stageright, unless by express contract stageright and copyright of the piece are sepa-

---

[1] 1867, 7 B. & T. 869; 10 L.R. Q.B. 347; *Sayer* v. *Dicey*, 1 Wils. 60; *Low* v. *Routledge*, 23 L.J. Ch. 717.

[2] Per Blackburn, J.

[3] 1864, 17 C.B. (N.S.) 419.

[4] 1834, 1 Ad. & E. 580; 3 N. & M. 537.

rated. The assignee under these circumstances may sue for penalties, although the assignment is not by deed or registered.

5 & 6 Vic. c. 45, § 2 enacts 'that the word "assigns" shall be construed to mean and include every person in whom the interest of an author in copyright shall be vested, whether derived from such author before or after the publication of any book, and whether acquired by sale, gift, bequest, or by operation of law, or otherwise.'

The question of what amounts to an assignment of stageright, and whether it need be in writing, has been raised somewhat frequently. In *Leader* v. *Purday*,[1] the author of a musical composition agreed in October 1844, by writing, not under seal, for the sale of his copyright to B, undertaking to execute, when called upon, a proper assignment to B, his executors &c., or as he or they should direct. It was held that this did not operate as an assignment to B, so as to render inoperative a subsequent regular assignment to B and C.

In *Lacy* v. *Toole*[2] the question was whether the terms of a letter amounted to an assignment of stageright. The letter ran thus:—' In answer to your letter of the 16th instant, I beg to say that I accept the offer you therein make me, and agree to the condition you propose for cancelling my debt to you, viz. to let you have my drama of "Doing for the Best" in discharge of 10*l*. of the sum due, and to furnish you with a little piece in a couple of months in payment of the balance.' This was held to be a complete assignment of his whole property in the drama. From this case it would appear that there is no prescribed mode of assignment for stageright, and that the assignment need not be in writing.

In *Levi* v. *Rutley*[3] the form of receipt would, it seems, have been sufficient, had the terms of it as to payment been complied with. See *Cumberland* v. *Copeland*, 1861. Ex. 7 H. & N. 118; 31 L. J. 19 Ex.; 4 L. T. (N. S.) 803.

[1] 1849, 7 C.B. 4.   [2] 1867, 15 L.T. (N.S.) 512.   [3] *Ante*, p. 66.

Whether *copyright* could be assigned otherwise than by writing was a question much discussed in early cases, and the doctrine established that it must be in writing, attested by two witnesses. In *Power* v. *Walker*,[1] Ellenborough, C.J., said that the Statutes of Anne having required the consent of the proprietor to the printing of his book to be in writing, it followed, *à fortiori*, that the assignment must also be. In *Clementi* v. *Walker*[2] it was held expressly that copyright would not pass by a verbal agreement. In *Rundell* v. *Murray*,[3] Eldon, C., was of the same opinion, although, as he remarked, it frequently happened that Courts of Equity granted injunctions at the suit of persons claiming under assignments not in writing. The later practice of this Court, when the defendant desired an action to be brought, was to impose on him the terms of admitting the plaintiff's legal title.

Stageright, like copyright,[4] will pass to a bankrupt's assignees.

V. INFRINGEMENT.

It is evident when we consider the nature of literary matter in general that the question whether the author of a work of fiction has made a fair use of another work, or has invaded the right in that work piratically, is very difficult to determine—more difficult beyond comparison than the same question with reference to the rights conferred by Letters Patent on an inventor.[5] In manufac-

---

[1] 4 Camp. 8; 3 Mau. & S. 7, *Latour* v. *Bland*; 2 Stark 382.
[2] 1824, 2 B. & Cr. 861; 4 Dowl. & Ry. 598.
[3] Jac. 311, *Davidson* v. *Bonn*, 1848; 6 C.B. 456.
[4] *Mawman* v. *Tegg* before Eldon, C.; 2 Russ. 385.
[5] The reader may consult on this head an able article 'On the Distinction between Copyright and Patent-right,' contained in a highly interesting compilation by Mr. Macfie, M.P., entitled 'Recent Discussions in the United Kingdom and on the Continent as to the Abolition of Patents.' Longman, 1869.

tures we may frequently determine the question by observing the similarity of result in the case of apparently different processes or different arrangement of machinery. In the case of a literary composition the analogy fails to be of service to us. The difficulty is, of course, only an additional reason for careful consideration in arriving at a conclusion, but all experience derived from decided cases proves that it is far easier to lay down general rules than to apply them. Cases of literary copyright are, of course, our chief guides, and to these I shall now refer.

That the system in vogue with us for determining the *fact* of literary piracy is the best possible for attaining that end may well be doubted; whether the author complained of has or has not infringed upon the rights of another author is indeed at times a question of such nicety as to be entirely unfit for submission to a jury.

In *Gyles* v. *Wilcox*,[1] a case before Lord Hardwicke in 1740, the facts of the case were certainly very formidable matter to lay before any jury. The question to be decided was whether 'The New Crown Law' was in substance the same as 'Hale's Pleas of the Crown.' His Lordship said, 'This, I think, is one of those cases where it would be much better for the parties to fix upon two persons of learning and abilities in the profession of the law, who would accurately and carefully compare them and report their opinion to the Court. The House of Lords very often in matters of account which are extremely perplexed and intricate, refer it to two merchants named by the parties to consider the case and report their opinion upon it rather than leave it to a jury, and I should think a reference of the same kind in some measure would be the properest method in the present case.'

It must be taken as decided beyond dispute that the question of representation is a question for the jury, and

[1] 2 Atk. 143.

where the jury decided[1] that the singing of two or three songs from an opera in the words of the plaintiff's version was a representation of part of it within the statute, and had given the lowest damages, the Court refused to disturb the verdict. In the case of *Toole* v. *Young* before referred to,[2] some little amusement was created at the trial when the question was discussed as to who was to read the rival performances in order to ascertain their identity. It was suggested by the Court that they should be read by Counsel, and Counsel suggested in reply that they should be read by an eminent comedian who happened to be present. They were eventually read by an officer of the Court.

Reference to some competent authority in Court is a common solution of the difficulty at *nisi prius*; the only one, in fact, that can be considered in any degree satisfactory.

How much may be taken without bringing the adapter within the law, and how little will serve to render him amenable to it, must in every case be left to be determined by the particular circumstances of that case. In *Bramwell* v. *Halcomb*,[3] Cottenham, C., said: 'One writer may take all the vital parts of another's book, though it might be but a small proportion of the book in quantity. In my view of the law Lord Eldon, in *Wilkins* v. *Aikin*,[4] put the question on a most proper footing. He says, "The question upon the whole is whether this is a legitimate use of the plaintiff's publication in the fair exercise of a mental operation deserving the character of an original work."'

The difference is not altogether unlike that between translations and translations referred to by Mr. Labouchere[5] on the introduction of the Bill of 1852: 'Trans

---

[1] *Planché* v. *Braham*, 1 Jur. 823; 8 C. and P. 68; 4 Bing. (N.S.) 17; *De Pinha* v. *Polhill*, 8 C. and P. 78.   [2] Ante, p. 21.

[3] 1836 (Copyright), 3 M. and Cr. 738. *Kelly* v. *Rooney*, 14 Jur., C. L. R. 158.

[4] 1810, 17 Ves. 422.   [5] 13 February, 1852, H. of Commons.

lations of works of imagination and poems,' he remarked, 'even of works of fiction—for instance, one of Sir Walter Scott's novels, must, it was clear, be very imperfect if they had not the merit of the original works. On the other hand, there was a class of works purely historical and scientific which had been translated by various persons in England, the translations of which were little more than mere reproductions of the original work by a merely mechanical operation.'

In *Carey* v. *Faden*,[1] Lord Loughborough refused an injunction to restrain the publication of an alleged piracy of Cary's Road Book, seemingly on the ground that a great part of the plaintiff's work was a copy of the preceding work of Patterson, in which the copyright had not yet expired; but from the general tenor of the case it is clear that a party has in such cases a copyright in his own additions, which has indeed been repeatedly decided with reference to the original work.

The abridgment must be a fair one, and not merely colorable; *Bell* v. *Walker*, 1 Bro. C. C.; *Butterworth* v. *Robinson*, 5 Ves. 709; *Pinnock* v. *Rose*, 2 Bro. 85; in note Ed. Belt *Longman* v. *Winchester*, 16 Ves. 269; *Matthewson* v. *Stockdale*, 12 Ves. 270; *Doddsley* v. *Kinnersley*, Amb. 403.

Publishing in the form of quadrilles and waltzes the airs of an opera in which there was copyright, was held to be piracy in *D'Almaine* v. *Boosey*,[2] in which case also it was held that publishing an original air, with adaptations and harmonies and for different instruments, was also piracy.[3]

In *Pike* v. *Nicholas*,[4] Hatherley, C., defines piracy as 'copying or copying with a colourable alteration.' In that case the plaintiff and defendant had published works

---

[1] 1799, 5 Ves. 24; *Cary* v. *Longman*, 1 East 357; cited in *Levy* v. *Rutley*, 1871; L. R. 6 C. P. 523; *Barfield* v. *Nicholson*, 2 S. and S. 1., 6.

[2] 1835, 1 Y. and C., Eq. Ex. 288.   [3] *Ibid.* 296.

[4] 1870, L. R., 5 Ch. 251.

on the same subject, the defendant referring to the plaintiff's book as one of the authorities he had consulted. With regard to the references which plaintiff adduced as proof of piracy, defendant stated that he had referred to the same authorities as the plaintiff, and showed that he had referred to two authorities not mentioned by the plaintiff, but as to two of the authorities referred to by the plaintiff and also by the defendant the defendant was unable to say where he had found them. It was held, by Hatherley, C., reversing a decision of James, V.C., that, under the circumstances, the defendant had not made such use of the plaintiff's book as to entitle the plaintiff to an injunction.

In *Boosey* v. *D'Almaine*,[1] it was held, that the adaptation of 'a considerable and recognisable part' of a melody was an infringement of the composer's right. In the course of the elaborate judgment delivered by Lyndhurst, C.B., in that case, his Lordship said: 'It is admitted that the defendant has published portions of the opera containing the melodious parts of it, that he has also published entire airs, and that in one of his waltzes he has introduced seventeen bars in succession, containing the whole of the original air, though he adds fifteen other bars which are not to be found in it. Now it is said that this is not a piracy because what the plaintiffs purchased was the entire opera, and the opera consists not merely of certain airs and melodies, but of the whole score. But in the first place, piracy may be of part of an air as well as the whole; and in the second place, admitting that the opera consists of the whole score, yet if the plaintiffs were entitled to the whole, *à fortiori* they were entitled to publish the melodies which form a part. Again, it is said that the present publication is adapted for dancing only, and that some degree of art is needed for the purpose of so adapting it, and that but a small part of the

---

[1] 1 Y. and C., Ex. Eq. 300.

merit belongs to the original composer. That is a nice question. It is a nice question what shall be deemed such a modification of an original work as shall absorb the merit of the original in the new composition. No doubt such a modification may be allowed in some cases, as in that of an abridgment or a digest. . . . A man may write upon morals in a manner quite different from that of others who preceded him, but the subject of music is to be regarded upon very different principles. It is the air or melody which is the invention of the author, and which may in such cases be the subject of piracy; and you commit a piracy if by taking not a single bar but several you incorporate in the new work, that on which the whole meritorious part of the invention consists. I remember in a case of copyright at *nisi prius* a question arising as to how many bars were necessary for the constitution of a subject or phrase. Sir George Smart, who was a witness in the case, said that a mere bar did not constitute a phrase, though three or four bars might do so. Now it appears to me, that if you take from the composition of an author all those bars consecutively which form the entire air or melody, without any material alteration, it is a piracy; though, on the other hand, you might take them in a different order, or, broken by the intersection of others, take words in such a manner as should not be a piracy. It must depend on whether the air taken is substantially the same with the original. Now the most unlettered in music can distinguish one song from another, and the mere adaptation of the air, either by changing it to a dance or by transferring it from one instrument to another, does not, even to common apprehensions, alter the original subject. The ear tells you that it is the same. The original air requires the aid of genius for its construction, but a mere mechanic in music can make the adaptation or accompaniment. Substantially the piracy is where the appropriated music, though adapted to a different purpose from that of the original, may still be recognised by the ear. The added variations make no difference in the principle.'

At times the matter presented for the consideration of the Court is complicated by the circumstance that the defendant's composition is really the plaintiff's composition, but after undergoing entire transmutations. In *Reade* v. *Lacy*,[1] the plaintiff sought to restrain the publication of the play, 'Never too Late to Mend.' The plaintiff was the originator of the composition. He published a play called 'Gold,' and subsequently a novel, 'It is Never too Late to Mend,' founded upon it. B. afterwards published a play compiled from the plaintiff's, without, as he alleged, any knowledge of the plaintiff's play. B.'s play contained scenes and passages substantially identical with scenes and passages which were common to both A.'s play and novel. *Held*, that even if B.'s play were a fair adaptation of the novel and not an infringement of the copyright therein,[2] it was an infringement of the copyright in the plaintiff's play; and the same would no doubt have been the decision had the suit been for the protection of plaintiff's stage-rights in his play.

There might, of course, be cases in which a close adherence to the plaintiff's plot with colourable [3] variations only in the dialogue, names of characters and scene would constitute what the law designates by the harsh name of Piracy: but it must be an extreme case in which this Court would interfere if its aid were invoked only by reason of the outline of a plot, however ingenious, having been taken. Of the plays of Shakspeare there is scarcely one of which the plot is not taken from stories already elaborated. Thus, his 'King John,' 'Richard II.,' 'Henry IV.' (both parts), 'Henry V.,' 'Richard III.,'

---

[1] 1861, 1 J. and H. 524.

[2] The fact that many of Sir Walter Scott's novels were dramatised without any objection on his part, was strongly urged upon the Court in *Tinsley* v. *Lacy*, 1863, 1 H. & M. 747.

[3] Note E, Appendix, 'Plagiarism.'

'Henry VIII.,' are taken from Holinshed's 'Chronicles;' incidents in 'King John,' 'Henry IV.,' and 'Henry V.' being taken from earlier plays of 'King John' and 'Henry V.;' 'Henry VI.' (three parts) are from 'Hall's Chronicle;' 'Macbeth' from Holinshed's 'History of Scotland.' Of 'King Lear' the historical part is from Holinshed, much of the matter from an old play of the same name and Sidney's 'Arcadia,' (Shakspeare probably also saw Higgins' 'Queen Cordila,' in the 'Mirror for Magistrates,') and so on.[1]

Whether a *fraudulent intent* on the defendant's part is necessary to induce the Court's interference by injunction has been much discussed, and may perhaps be still considered an open question; but there can be no doubt that disingenuous statements in the defendant's answer influence the Court strongly in coming to the conclusion that the use made of the plaintiff's work has not been 'a fair use.'

Servile copying of parts of a work; although other parts of it may be different, have on this principle, from very early times, been held piracy. *Trusler* v. *Murray*, 1 East 363; *Thompson* v. *Stanhope*, Amb. 737; *Jeffreys* v. *Baldwin*, Amb. 164. 'The question I really have to try,' said Wood V.C. in *Jerrold* v. *Houlston*,[2] 'is whether the use that has in this case been made of the plaintiff's book has gone beyond a fair use. Now, for trying that question several tests have been laid down: one, which was originally expressed, I think, by a common-law judge, and was adopted by Lord Langdale in *Lewis* v. *Fullarton*,[3] is whether you find on the part of the defendant an *animus furandi*, an intention to take for the purpose of saving himself labour.' The defendant having in that case denied

---

[1] For a collection of the romances, novels, poems, and histories used by Shakspeare as the foundation for such of his dramas as are not derived from Greek, or Roman, or English history, or were not formed upon some earlier play, see Shakspeare's Library, published by Payne Collier, 1843; Thomas Rodd, London.

[2] 1857, 3 K. and J., 716; 3 Jur. (N.S.), 1051.   [3] 2 Beav. 6.

having copied or taken any idea or language from the plaintiff's work, was held a strong indication of his *animus furandi*.

In *Scott* v. *Sandford*,[1] a different doctrine was acted on by the same learned Judge, who held that the result in such cases is the true test of the act; and full acknowledgment of the original, and the absence of any dishonest intention, will not excuse the appropriator, when the effect of his appropriation is of necessity to injure and supersede the sale of the original work.

The subject of Titles of plays has been before adverted to. They form so important a feature in registration of stageright and copyright as to suggest much caution in their selection. The reasoning in *Chappell* v. *Sheard*[2] (a case of copyright) seems to be applicable to this subject. In that case certain music publishers having adapted original words to an old American air which was rearranged for them, gave to the song so composed the name of 'Minnie,' and procured it to be sung by a popular singer, at Julien's concerts, in London. When it had by that means become a favourite song they published it with a title-page, containing a picture of the singer, and the words ' "Minnie"; sung by Madame Annie Thillon and Miss Dolby at Julien's concerts; written by George Linley, &c.' It was held that the publishers had by these means obtained a right of property in that name and description of their song, which a Court of Equity would restrain any person from infringing.

Another music publisher subsequently published the same melody with different words, and upon the title-page placed a similar portrait, with the words ' "Minnie Dale"; sung at Jullien's concerts, and always encored, by Madame Annie Thillon; the music composed by H. S. Thompson, &c.,' this song never having, in truth, been

---

[1] 1867 (Copyright), 3 L. R. Eq. 718.
[2] 1855, 2 K. and J. 117; *Chappell* v. *Davidson*, 2 K. and J. 123.

sung by Madame Annie Thillon at Julien's concerts. The defendant was enjoined, this being a palpable attempt to induce the public to believe that the song so published was the same as that of the first publishers.

In interfering by way of injunction in cases of titles, the Court acts on the principle of preventing mistakes on the part of the public as to what work is really intended by it. This was the principle laid down in *Clement* v. *Maddick*. 'It appears to me,' observed Wood, V.C., in *Kelly* v. *Hutton*,[1] 'that there is nothing analogous to copyright in the name of a newspaper, but that the proprietor has a right to prevent any other person from adopting the same name for any similar publication.'[2]

VI. PROCEEDINGS AGAINST INFRINGERS.

5 & 6 Vic. c. 45, § 21 gives to the proprietors of the right of dramatic representation or musical performance during the term of their interest, all the remedies provided by 3 & 4 Will. IV. c. 15, the provisions of which we have already considered. The proprietor can either sue for penalties at Law or for an injunction and account in Equity.

The jurisdiction of Equity as regards literary piracy is assumed[3] merely for the purpose of giving effect to the legal right which cannot be made effectual by any action for damages, and, therefore, before the Court will interfere it must be satisfied either by the result of a trial at law or by evidence showing a strong probability that an action would be successful, if brought, that the plaintiff has a legal title, or a title only defective at law by reason

---

[1] Sec. 1 Giff., 98; 5 Jur. (N.S.), 592.
[2] 1868, 3 L. R. Ch., App.
[3] 2 Story Eq. Jur. 209. The remedy at law by action on the case given by the statute does not exclude the equitable jurisdiction; *Sheriff* v. *Coates*, 1 Russ. and M. 159.

of some technical objection. 'This Court,' observed Cottenham C., in *Saunders* v. *Smith*,[1] 'exercises its jurisdiction not for the purpose of acting upon legal rights, but for the purpose of better enforcing legal rights or preventing mischief until they have been ascertained. In all cases of injunctions in aid of legal rights, whether it be copyright, patent right,[2] or some other description of legal right which comes before this Court, the office of the Court is consequent upon the legal right, and it generally happens that the only question the Court has to consider is whether the case is so clear and so free from objection, upon the grounds of equitable consideration, that the Court ought to interfere by injunction without a previous trial at law, or whether it ought to wait till the legal title has been established. The distinction depends upon a great variety of circumstances, and it is utterly impossible to lay down any general rule upon the subject by which the discretion of the Court ought, in all cases, to be regulated.'

Suits for injunction should be instituted as soon as possible after the discovery of the infringement.[3] Acquiescence in infringement will disentitle a party aggrieved to the assistance of the Court by interlocutory injunction (*The Correspondent Co.* v. *Saunders*).[4]

The Court does not require all the parties legally entitled to be before it.[5] The title of one of several joint authors would appear to be sufficient to support the bill.[6]

The general course of proceeding in Equity to restrain infringement of stageright is similar to that involved in cases of patents for inventions [7] and copyright.

[1] 3 My. and Cr. 728.
[2] See as to the practice with reference to Patents, Coryton on Patents, 'Remedies for Infringement.'
[3] *Chappell* v. *Sheard*, 1855, 2 K. and J. 117.
[4] 1865, 12 L. T. (N.S.) 540; 11 Jur. (N.S.) 540; 13 W. R. 804. *Platt* v. *Button*, 19 Ves. 447.
[5] *Sweet* v. *Cater*, 5 Jur. 68.   [6] *Mawman* v. *Tegg*, 2 Russ. 385.
[7] See Coryton on Patents, 318-346, 'On the remedy of the Patentee by bill in Equity.'

Owing to the peculiar circumstances of theatrical management some difficulty is at times experienced in selecting the proper party for a defendant.

In *Lyon* v. *Knowles*[1] the defendants, the proprietors of a theatre, allowed one Dillon the use of it for dramatic entertainments. The defendants provided the band (music being a necessary part of the performance), the scene-shifters, the supernumeraries, the money-takers, and paid for printing and advertising. Dillon employed his own company for acting, and selected the pieces for representation independently of the defendant. The money taken was shared equally by the defendant and Dillon. Under these circumstances certain pieces were performed, of which the plaintiff had the sole right of representation as assignee of the author, under the Dramatic Literary Property Acts, 3 & 4 Will. IV. c. 15, and 5 & 6 Vic. c. 45. It was held that no action under those statutes was maintainable against the defendant, as the facts did not show that the pieces had been represented by him, or that there was a partnership between him and Dillon, so as to render him liable for the representation of them by Dillon.

In *Russell* v. *Briant*[2] it was held that the landlord of a tavern, who let it for the evening for the public performance of songs and music, and provided lights, benches, &c., was not liable.

In *Marsh* v. *Conquest*,[3] the defendant, the proprietor of a theatre, let it for one night for the benefit of one of his performers, who was to pay 30*l.* for the use of the theatre, with the services of the *corps dramatique*, band, lights, and accessories. The performer having acted a piece the stageright of which was in the plaintiff, it

---

[1] 1863, 11 W. R. 266; 3 B. and S. 556; 5 B. and S. 751; 12 W. R. 1083; 10 L. T. (N.S.) 876.

[2] 19 L. J., C.P., 33; 14 Jur. (N.S.) 201; 8 C.B. 836. In the judgment in this case the word 'copyright' was used by Wilde, C.J., to denote the right infringed.

[3] 1864, 17 C.B. (N.S.) 419.

was held that the defendant was liable in an action for penalties.

A question somewhat similar had arisen before the Dramatic Copyright Act in *qui tam* actions for penalties under 10 Geo. II. c. 28.[1] In *Parsons* v. *Chapman*[2] proof that a party was the acting manager of a theatre, and that he paid the salary of and dismissed one of the actors, was held sufficient proof that he caused the performance, and if he caused the performance, it was said it was not material whether he did so as the agent of others or not. Allegation in the declaration in the terms of the statute that the plaintiff has the sole liberty of representing a certain musical composition is a sufficient statement of the plaintiff's right in an action for penalties.[3]

The bill for an injunction must state the title of the plaintiff, the circumstances of the piracy, and the injury consequent upon it. Injury being proved in the case of *Tinsley* v. *Lacy*,[4] Wood, V.C., said: 'I do not think I should be justified in sending the case to a jury to determine whether any damages have been incurred; and, as to the law, I am bound to decide that myself. It would, in any case, be extremely difficult to measure the amount of injury done to an author by a publication of this kind. The account being waived, the decree will simply be for a perpetual injunction.'

If a part of a play only be pirated, the bill should distinguish that part; otherwise costs unnecessarily incurred must be borne by the plaintiff.[5]

'The quantity pirated ought to be ascertained,' said Eldon, C., in *Mawman* v. *Tegg*,[6] 'in order to authorise the Court to say that no part of the piratical work should go on; and on the other hand, nothing is more difficult than

---

[1] Repealed by 6 and 7 Vic., c. 68, s. 1.
[2] 1831, 5 C. and P. 33.
[3] *Russell* v. *Smith*, 17 L. J., Q.B., 225.
[4] 1864 (Copyright), 1 H. and M. 754.
[5] *Page* v. *Wisden*, 1869 (Copyright), 17 W. R., 483; 20 L. J. (N.S.) 435.
[6] 1826 (Copyright), 2 Russ. 398.

to grant an injunction against part of a work, although an action may be brought for pirating a part. It appears to have been Lord Hardwicke's opinion,[1] that an injunction might be granted against the whole, although only part was pirated.' His Lordship referred to another case (probably *Cary* v. *Longman*, 1 East 360, and *Trusler* v. *Murray*, 1 East 363), tried before Lord Kenyon, in which an opinion laid down by Lord Bathurst was approved,— namely, that an injunction could not issue against the whole, 'unless the part pirated was such, that granting an injunction against that part necessarily destroyed the whole.'

The author may, as we have seen, assign his stageright without such assignment being by deed or registered under 5 & 6 Vic. c. 45, so as to enable his assignee to sue for penalties;[2] but where the plaintiff derived his title by assignment in the book of register from a proprietor whose title was not registered according to the Act, a demurrer was allowed.

Every application for an injunction before answer must be accompanied by an affidavit of merits, verifying the material statements of the bill.[3]

A plaintiff has a right to a full and particular discovery as to the original sources from which the defendant alleges himself to have drawn his work. In a suit to restrain infringement of copyright,[4] James, V.C., said, 'If I charge you with having taken information from my book, and you derived your information from original sources, I have a right to know what those original sources were.'

In *Bacon* v. *Jones*,[5] a case of infringement of a patent, the principles upon which the Court bases its interference were thus generally stated by Cottenham, C. 'When a

---

[1] 4 Burr. 2326.

[2] *Marsh* v. *Conquest*, 10 Jur. (N.S.) 989; *Low* v. *Routledge*, 10 Jur. (N.S.) 922; 33 L. J. Ch. 717; 12 W. R. 1069; 10 L. T. (N.S.) 838.

[3] See the cases cited in Coryton on Patents, 324.

[4] *Kelly* v. *Wyman*, 1869, 17 W. R. 399.

[5] 1839, 4 My. & Cr., 436.

party applies for the aid of the Court, the application for an injunction is made either during the progress of the suit or at the hearing, and in both cases I apprehend great latitude and discretion are allowed to the Court in dealing with the application. When the application is for an interlocutory injunction several courses are open. The Court may at once grant the injunction *simpliciter* without more, a course which, though perfectly competent to the Court, is not very likely to be taken when the defendant raises a question as to the validity of the plaintiff's title; or it may follow the more usual and, as I apprehend, the more wholesome practice in such a case of either granting an injunction and at the same time directing the plaintiff to proceed to establish his legal title, or of requiring him first to establish his title at law, and suspending the grant of the injunction until the result of the legal investigation has been ascertained, the defendant in the meantime keeping an account. Which of these several courses ought to be taken must depend entirely upon the discretion of the Court, according to the case made.'

As a rule the Court requires, in cases in application for *ex parte* injunctions, the plaintiff to make oath that he is the proprietor of the right. In *Butterworth* v. *Robinson*,[1] 5 Vic. 709, the injunction appears to have been granted on certificate of bill filed. See on this head the cases cited in the notes to Jarman & Bythewood Precedents, 3 Ed. 663.

If the defendant admit the plaintiff's title and the infringement, an injunction will at once issue. The plaintiff is entitled after such admission, even if the defendant undertake that there shall be no further infringement, to the usual order for an injunction.[2]

---

[1] *Percival* v. *Phipps*, 2 Ves. and Bea. 26; *Gee* v. *Pritchard*, 2 Swans. 406; *Wyatt* v. *Burnard*, 3 Ves. and B.
[2] *Losh* v. *Hague*, 2 Cooper, C. C. 59 n.

The usual course when the Court is not satisfied as to the plaintiff's title or the fact of infringement, is to grant an injunction pending the trial of the right at law, or direct the motion to stand over till the hearing, on the terms of the defendant keeping an account.

The statements in the particulars of objection must be as full as the defendant's means of information enable him to make them.[1] In an action on the case for an infringement of copyright the defendant pleaded several pleas denying that the plantiff was the proprietor of the copyright, that there was any copyright subsisting, that the books were first published in England, and that the copies complained of were unlawfully printed. Held on application by the plaintiff to have the notice of objections delivered with the defendant's pleas, under 5 & 6 Vic. c. 45, § 16, amended, that the alleged first publication having taken place abroad, and so far back as the year 1831, it was sufficient for the defendant to state the year of the first publication, and that it was not necessary that he should specify the day and month.

But that he was bound to state the name of the party whom he alleged to be the proprietor, or first publisher, the title of the work, the place where, and the time when, the first publication took place.

Held, also, that he was not entitled to object that 'some person whose name is to the defendant unknown and not the plaintiff' was the proprietor of the said copyright; nor 'that the plaintiff himself was not the author;' nor 'that the work was not first printed or published in the British dominions;' nor that the plaintiff never acquired any title by assignment ' or otherwise ' to the copyright; nor that there was no 'valid' assignment, &c.; nor 'that there is no copyright in a work first published out of the British dominions under such circumstances as the books

---

[1] *Boosey* v. *Davidson*, 1846, 4 D. and L. 147.

in question were published,' but that he might object 'that A. B., if any one, and not the plaintiff,' was the proprietor; and that at the time of committing the alleged grievances no 'copyright' in the work 'was existing.'

Ignorance of the plaintiff's rights is, of course, no defence to an action for infringement. 'The plaintiff's rights do not depend upon the innocence or guilt of the defendant . . . . . The statute would altogether fail to effect its object if it were necessary to show that the defendant had a knowledge of the plaintiff's right of property.'[1]

We have already noticed the subject of evidence in cases of infringement.[2] In cases of copyright the usual course was formerly to refer the publications to the Master for comparison, *Jeffrey* v. *Bowles*, 1769, Dick. 429; *Carnan* v. *Bowles*, 1786, 2 Bro. C. C. 80; ——— v. *Leadbetter*, 1799, 4 Ves. 681. Sometimes, however, the Court undertook the decision of the question of piracy itself, *Whittingham* v. *Wooler*, 2 Swans. 428; *Sheriff* v. *Coates*, 1 R. & M. 149. In the important case of *Lewis* v. *Fullarton*, 2 Beav. 6; Lord Langdale, M.R., read a considerable number of articles in both works, with a view of determining the identity. See also *Jarrold* v. *Houlston*, 1857, 3 K. & J. 716. The present practice is for the Judge to compare the books in Court, with the assistance of Counsel, or at home.

In some cases presumption of *mala fides* has been admitted from the circumstances of the case. In *Byron* v. *Johnston*[3] a bill was filed on behalf of Lord Byron, to restrain the defendant in respect of certain poems he had advertised for sale as Lord Byron's poems. An injunction issued until answer or further order to restrain the publication of the work as the plaintiff's, upon affidavit of the plaintiff's agents (the plaintiff being himself

---

[1] Per Wilde, C.J., *Lee* v. *Simpson*, 1847, 3 C.B. 871.   [2] Ante, p. 83.
[3] 1816, 2 Mer 29. See *Abernethy* v. *Hutchinson*, 3 L. J. 209 Ch.; 1 H. and T. 39.

abroad) of circumstances making it highly probable that it was not the plaintiff's work, and the defendant refusing to swear to his belief that it was so.

From *Wood* v. *Chart*[1] it would appear that a Court of Equity will go into evidence to see whether the registered version of a translation under the International Copyright Acts is a true translation.

Where an injunction is granted restraining the publication and sale of a work pending a trial at law to determine the question of alleged piracy, it is not necessary that the order should specify the particular articles alleged to have been pirated, although the plaintiffs do not claim copyright on the whole of the articles contained in their publication, it being admitted that some of the articles in the two works had been derived from a source common both to the plaintiffs and defendants; nor are the plaintiffs in such a case, in order to support the injunction, bound to specify particularly in what articles they claim the copyright.[2]

Where the plaintiff is entitled to a perpetual injunction he is entitled to an account, and the smallness of the injury will not protect the defendant from having to pay costs unless he has offered, on the injunction being granted to pay the costs up to that time.[3]

The principle upon which the court gives an account in cases of piracy, was thus stated by Wigram, V.C., in *Colburn* v. *Simms*.[4] The court by the account, as the nearest which it can make to parties, takes away from the wrongdoer all the profits he has made by his piracy, and gives them to the party who has been wronged. In doing this the Court may often give the injured party more than in fact he is entitled to for *non constat* that a single additional copy of the more expensive book would have been

---

[1] 10 L. R. Ch. 202.
[2] *Sweet* v. *Maugham*, 1840, 9 L. J.(N.S.) 323.
[3] *Fradella* v. *Weller*, 1831, 2 Russ. and M. 247.
[4] 1843, 2 Hare 554.

sold, if the injury by the sale of the cheaper book had not been committed. The circumstances of stage-right are different, no doubt; but the argument would seem to be applicable to a piratical representation of a stage-play.

The defendant will have to account for every representation, and pay the profits of those representations to the plaintiff.[1] As a general rule, penalties and forfeitures must be waived by a party seeking equitable relief.[2]

It is not necessary in the case of bankruptcy of a plaintiff pending judgment to revive.[3]

Costs in Equity are in the discretion of the Court. The Court will not make an order for costs where it is probable that proceedings may afterwards take place which will affect the decision of the Court on the question of costs.[4] If defendant offers to submit to injunction and pay costs, and the plaintiff bring the cause to a hearing, the Court will give the defendant subsequent costs.[5] It would appear from *Upman v. Elkan*[6] that there may be circumstances under which, even in the case of a plaintiff's title having been taken, the defendant would not have to pay the plaintiff's costs.

In *Boucicault* v. *Delafield*[7] the plaintiff, after the hearing but before judgment was delivered, became bankrupt. The bill was dismissed, and the defendant moved that the plaintiff might be ordered personally to pay the costs. Wood, V.C., refused to make any order, and his decision[8] was upheld on appeal.

---

[1] *Pike* v. *Nicholas*, 1870, L. R. 5 Ch. 251.
[2] *Colburn* v. *Simms* (sup.) [3] *Boucicault* v. *Delafield*, 9 Jur. (N.S.) 1282.
[4] See the cases cited Joyce on Injunctions, 255.
[5] *Moet* v. *Couston*, 33 Beav. 578; 10 Jur. (N.S.) 1012; 10 L. T. (N.S.) 395.
[6] 20 W. R. 131; L. R., 12 Eq. 140; 19 W. R. 867.
[7] 1864, 10 Jur. (N.S.) 1063. [8] *Ibid*. 937.

Appendix.

Note A.—The Drama.

The word drama is Greek. It signifies in English, a poem accommodated to action; a poem in which the action is not related, but represented.—*Todd's Johnson,* 'Drama.'

On the extreme antiquity of this form of literature it is needless to enlarge. It is probably as old as literature itself. The Book of Job, as has been pointed out by a very eminent writer, 'presents us in a dramatised form with a history of a man, the specimen of humanity, struggling under an overpowering weight of calamity to discover the cause of human misery, how its existence is compatible with the mercy of God, the sense of inward evil fighting against the feeling that in some sense he is a righteous man, surviving amidst patient hope, doubt, and despondency.'—*Encyc. Brit.* ii. 564, Art. 'Drama.'

'However general,' observes Sir Walter Scott, 'the predisposition to the assumption of fictitious characters may be, there is an immeasurable distance between the rude games in which it first displays itself and that polished amusement which is numbered among the fine arts, which poetry, music, and painting, have vied to adorn, and to whose service genius has devoted her most sublime efforts, whilst philosophy has stooped from her loftiest task to regulate the progress of the action and give probability to the representation and personification of the scene.'

'The history of Greece—of that wonderful country, whose days of glory have left such a never-dying blaze of radiance behind them . . . affords us the means of tracing the polished and well-regulated drama, the subject of severe rule, and the vehicle for expressing the noblest poetry from amusements as rude in their outline as the mimic sports of children or savages. The history of the Grecian stage is that of the dramatic art. . . They transferred the drama, with their other literature, to the victorious Romans, with whom it rather existed as a foreign than flourished as a native art. Like the other fine arts, the stage sunk under the decay of the empire, and its fall was accelerated by the introduction of the Christian religion. In the Middle Ages dramatic representation revived in the shape of the homely mysteries and moralities of our forefathers. The revival of letters threw light upon the scenic art, by making us acquainted with the pitch of perfection to which it had been carried by the genius of Greece. With this period commences the history of the modern stage, properly so called.'—*Encyc. Brit.* Art. 'Drama.'

For a very learned and interesting history of the ancient drama, from its origin in the rude revelry and fantastic mummeries of shepherds and peasants at their village festival of Bacchus to the days of Æschylus, the reader is referred to Potter's 'Antiquities of Greece.' See also Smith's 'Classical Dictionary,' and Donaldson's 'History and Exhibition of the Greek Drama.'

From such materials as rude songs, coarse jests, and here and there the recital by some strolling bard of popular fables or Homeric poems—it occurred some time about 535 B.C. (Donaldson's 'Chronology of the Greek Drama,' p. 205) to one Thespis, a native of Attica, to take the first step towards the establishment of what we may call dramatic entertainment. The great idea of this first of theatrical managers was to isolate the performers, who till now had run riot in the crowd, and place them on a planked platform built upon a cart, from which vantage ground, like the mountebanks of modern times, they amused the people.

The stage once raised, the genius of the people did the rest, and dramatic art at Athens was pushed on quickly to perfection. To the dull monotony of the Thespian orator succeeded at a bound, as it were, the magnificent performances of Æschylus, where noble diction, well regulated music, scenery, and dress afforded every accessory requisite to heighten the illusion of the scene, while—greatest marvel perhaps of all the marvels achieved by this strangely-gifted man—'a theatre circumscribed, whilst it accommodated the spectators, and reduced a casual and disorderly mob to the quality and civilisation of a regular and attentive audience...... The personal disguise which had been formerly attained by staining the actor's face was now by what doubtless was considered as a high exertion of ingenuity, accompanied by the use of a mask so painted as to represent the personage which he performed.'—*Sir W. Scott.*

To Æschylus succeeded Euripides and Sophocles, and tragedy and comedy began to run each its separate course. Both, as Aristotle bids us remark, 'owe almost their existence to the fruitful genius of Homer, the "Iliad" and the "Odyssey" furnishing subjects and characters for tragedy, and his poem of "Margites" for comedy. In the two former poems there is an astonishing variety of action animated and interesting in the highest degree. All the passions are painted in the strongest colours. Characters are drawn and supported with the utmost discrimination and correctness, and dramatic scenes are represented with all the truth and simplicity of nature. They furnish also in the unity and probability of the subject, in the different characters of the actors, in the sentiments they utter upon particular occasions, in the conduct of the story, and the issue of the whole, the germ and outlines of tragedy. It was unquestionably from meditating upon these great models with the mind of a philosopher, that Æschylus formed the idea of giving to tragedy the form in which she is seen in his works. He himself declared that his tragedies were but scraps from the magnificent repasts of Homer. The improvements he made on the drama were the following,—instead of one actor or interlocutor he introduced two upon a stage adorned with scenery corresponding to the situation in which the plot was laid.—*Potter's Ant. Gr.*, 'Short History of Grecian Literature,' p. 76.

The first play of Aristophanes was put upon the stage 383 B.C.—*Donaldson*. Of the works of other comedians we possess only detached fragments, but eleven of the plays of this great writer have come down to us complete. Of the 105 or 108 (*Donaldson*, p. 200) comedies of Menander, a few fragments only remain, and we are left to judge of his productions from those of his great imitator, Terence.

Dramatic entertainments found their way to Rome in the year of the city's founding, 391, when there was a desire to propitiate the Divine Being who had visited it with a plague. Till that date they had only, we are told, the circus games.—*Ov. de Art. Am.* i. 105; *Serv. in Virg.* i. 164; *Suet. Tib.* 34; *Cic. Planc.* 11; *Verr.* iii. 79; *Suet. Cæs.* 84. The plays acted were borrowed from Etruria, as was also the word to designate the actor *histrio* from an Etruscan word *hister.*—*Liv.* vii. 2.

Euripides and Sophocles had been dead for upwards of a century and a half, and Menander above half a century before (B.C. 240) the first writer, one Livius Andronicus, of a regular play arose at Rome. Plays were afterwards framed upon this model of, or as we should say 'adapted from,' the Greek by Nævius, Plautus, Cæcilius, Terence, Afranius, Pacuvius, Accius and others. Of these Nævius, Afranius, Plautus, Cæcilius, and Terence copied chiefly from Menander, 'the best writer of comedies that ever existed.'—*Quintilian*, x. 1.

No Roman tragedies have come down to us, excepting a few bearing the name of Seneca, and the only extant works of the comedians are those of Plautus and Terence.

See on the subject of the stage at Rome the chapter

in 'Donaldson,' p. 306, 'On the Roman Theatre' founded on Schlegel's Eighth Lecture.

Pantomimes are said to have been the invention of Augustus, although before his time the *mimi* both spoke and acted. The most celebrated composers of mimical performances were Laberius and Publius Syra, in the times of Julius Cæsar. The most famous under Augustus were Pylades and Bathyllus, between whom a strong rivalry existed, which carried their respective admirers to the length of bloodshed.—*Potter's Gr. Ant.*

In what are known as the Dark Ages that succeeded, we find here and there a rude drama springing up among the people, which, like the drama of the Greeks, had its origin in religious rites, 'with this great difference, that as the rites of Bacchus before and even after the improvements introduced by Thespis were well enough suited to the worship of such a Deity, the religious dramas, mysteries, or whatever other name they assumed, were often so unworthy of the Christian religion on which they were founded, that their being tolerated can only be attributed to the gross ignorance of the laity and the cunning of the Catholic priesthood, who used them with other idle and sometimes indecorous solemnities as one means of amusing men's minds and detaining them in contented bondage to their spiritual superiors.'—*Encyc. Brit.* Art. ' Drama.'

As to the country in which these representations of religious dramas first made their appearance antiquarians are not agreed. 'The practice of processions and pageants with music, in which characters, chiefly of Sacred Writ, were presented before the public, is so immediately connected with that of speaking exhibitions, that it is difficult to discrimiuate the one from the other. In Italy, Walker, in his 'Essay on the Revival of the Drama in Italy' (p. 6), informs us, the first speaking drama, 'Della Passione di nostro Signor Giesù Christo,' was written by Guiliano Dati, Bishop of San Leo, who flourished about 1445. The French drama is traced by M. Legrand as high as the thirteenth century, and he has produced one curious example of a pastoral, entitled 'Un Jeu.' He mentions also a farce, two devotional pieces, and two moralities, to each of which he ascribes the same title.

At a still earlier date, the religious play would seem to have been well established in this country. The 'Chester Mysteries,' or 'Whitsun Plays' as they were called, having been performed during the mayoralty of John Arneway, who filled the office at Chester from 1268 to 1276.

To the 'Mysteries' succeeded the 'Moralities,' a species of dramatic exercise which involved more art and ingenuity, and was besides much more proper for a public amusement than the imitations or rather parodies of sacred history, which had hitherto entertained the public. These moralities bear some analogy to the old or original comedy of the ancients. They were often founded upon allegorical subjects, and almost always bore a close and pregnant allusion to the incidents of the day.

'The difference between the Catholic and reformed religion was fiercely disputed in some of these "Moralities," and in Scotland in particular a mortal blow was aimed at the superstitions of the Roman Church by the celebrated Sir David Lindsay, in a play or morality acted in 1539, and entitled "The Satire of the Three Estates." The objects of the drama were entirely political, although it is mixed with some comic scenes, and introduced by an interlude in coarseness altogether unmatched. The spirit of Aristophanes, in all its good and evil, seems to have actuated the Scottish king-at-arms.'—*Encyc. Brit.*

While the learned at this period were labouring to revive the classical drama, the public at large became devoted to a species of representation which has been termed historical drama, and which properly fell neither within the denomination of tragedy or comedy. The dramatic chronicles, therefore, were a field in which the genius of the poet laboured to supply, by characters, sentiment, and incident, the meagre detail of the historian. They became so popular in England, that during the short interval betwixt the revival of the stage and the appearance of Shakspeare, the most part of the English monarchs had lived and died upon the stage; and it is well known that almost all his historical plays were new written by him upon the plan of old dramatic chronicles which already existed.

'The drama proper of England commences upon a Spanish model. "Ferrex and Porrex" was the first composition approaching to a regular tragedy. It was acted before Queen Elizabeth, the 15th January, 1561, by the gentlemen of the Inner Temple. It partakes rather of the character of a historical than of a classical drama, although more nearly allied to the latter class than the chronicle plays which afterwards took possession of the stage. English comedy, considered as a regular composition, may be considered to begin with "Gammer Gurton's Needle," acted at Christchurch College, Cambridge, 1575.

'These models were followed by a variety of others. Numerous theatres sprang up in different parts of the metropolis, opened upon speculation by distinct troops of performers. They acted under licenses which appear to have been granted for the purpose of police alone, not of exclusive privilege or monopoly, since London contained in the latter part of the sixteenth century no fewer than fourteen distinct companies of players, with very considerable privileges and remunerations.' (See 'Drake's Shakspeare and his Times,' ii. 205.)

'The players and dramatists before the rise of Shakspeare, following the taste of the public, dealt in the surprising, elevating, and often bombastic incidents of tragedy, as well as in the low humour and grotesque incidents of the comic scenes. When these singly were found to lack attraction, they mingled them together, and dashed their tragic plot with an under-intrigue of the lowest buffoonery, without any respect to taste or congruity.

'The English stage may be considered as equally without rule and without model until Shakspeare arose . . . Fortunately for the full exertion of a genius as comprehensive and versatile as intense and powerful, Shakspeare had no access to any models of which the commanding merit might have controlled and limited his own exertions. He followed the path which a nameless crowd of obscure writers had trodden before him, but he moved in it with the grace and majestic step of a being of a superior order, and vindicated for ever the British theatre from a pedantic restriction to classical rule. Nothing went before Shakspeare which in any respect was fit to fix and stamp the character of a national drama: certainly no one will succeed him capable of establishing by mere authority a form more restricted than that which Shakspeare used.' —*Encyc. Brit.* Art. Drama.

Much valuable and interesting information as to the origin, state, and prospects of our drama, stage, and its professors will be found in 'Henslowe's Diary,' published by the Shakspeare Society, and in Collier's History of English Dramatic Poetry, 3 vols., 1831.

NOTE B.—AUTHORS' REMEDIES AT LAW.

The fundamental changes now contemplated in the constitution and practice of our Courts of Law, may perhaps excuse my using this case in illustration of the advantages that would accrue to authors, patentees, and others, from a fusion of Law and Equity, and the adoption of a Code such as in a very imperfect but still serviceable form has been for many years in use in India. The plaintiff was here complaining that the defendant had infringed his right of representation on the stage. What he wanted was compensation for the past and protection for the future. Had such a case been tried in Calcutta or Madras the Court would have given the plaintiff a decree for his damages and enjoined the defendant. Act VIII. of 1859 (of India), § 93, provides that ' in any suit for restraining the defendant from the committal of any breach of contract or other injury, and whether the same be accompanied with any claim to damages or not, it shall be lawful for the plaintiff, at any time after the commencement of the suit, and whether before or after judgment, to apply to the Court for an injunction to restrain the defendant from the repetition or the continuance of the breach of contract or wrongful act complained of, or the committal of any breach of contract or injury of a like kind arising out of the same contract, or relating to the same property or right; and such injunction may be granted by the Court on such terms, as to the duration of the injunction, keeping an account, giving security or otherwise, as to such Court shall seem reasonable and just, and in case of disobedience such injunction may be enforced by imprisonment in the same manner as a decree for specific performance. Provided always that any order for an injunction may be discharged or set aside by the Court on application made thereto by any party dissatisfied with such order.' See as to the equitable power of Courts of Law at home, 17 & 18 Vict. c. 125.

I would note, as bearing on the same subject, that under a Civil Procedure Code such as that of India' *the Court* would, even if by a mistake in the pleadings the plaintiff had not raised this point, have raised it and decided it if it was material to the administration of justice. For in India the *onus* of seeing that the parties are placed at issue on the merits of a case is on the Court. By sec. 139 of Act VIII. of 1859, the Court at the first hearing of the suit shall 'enquire and ascertain upon what questions of law or fact the parties are at issue, and shall thereupon proceed to frame and record the issues of law and fact upon which the right decision of the case may depend. The Court may frame the issues from the allegations of fact which it collects from the oral examination of the parties or their pleaders, notwithstanding any difference between such allegations of fact and the allegations of fact contained in the written statements, if any, tendered by the parties or their pleaders.'

As regards Bentham's epithet of 'Judge-made law,' Wharton (Law Lex.:' Tit. Judge-made Law') observes, 'This phrase is applied as a term of reproach to decisions in which the bench is thought to have stepped beyond its proper province in introducing new principles. But it is clear that in declaring the law, the judges must often, while acting constitutionally, do what is practically equivalent to making law.'

Note C.—Remuneration of Authors.

Playgoing, after the modern fashion, may be said to have existed in ancient Greece, but the receipts and disbursements of the play at Athens were arranged upon very different principles to those obtaining in the management of theatres at the present day. The spectators paid for admission, it is true, but the theatre was strongly subsidised, and formed the subject of anxious care on the part of the highest functionaries of the State. The price of admission, we are told, was at first one drachma (according to Dr. Arbuthnot's Tables, about $7\frac{1}{2}d$.); but Pericles, courting popularity, reduced it to a third of that sum, or two oboli. To fill up the deficit created, the great statesman had recourse to a fund which had been set aside to sustain the expenses of the war. It is said of this great demagogue by Plutarch that he courted the people, 'and endeavoured to ingratiate himself with them, contriving to have always some show or play, or feast or procession, in the city, and to amuse them with the politest pleasures.'

Under circumstances so dissimilar to those of the present day, it is useless to seek for anything resembling the property a modern author claims as stage-right, or speculate, except as a matter of antiquarian interest, upon the earnings of the predecessors of the dramatic author of to-day. In the early days of Greece and Rome the philosopher, the orator, and the poet seem to have trusted for their remuneration to the liberality of their patrons, whether potentates or public audiences. Terence, indeed, as we learn from the prologue to one of them,[1] sold his plays to the Roman Ædiles, and Juvenal[2] gives an account of a similar sale by Statius. The former instance is curious, as indicating a complaint not unheard of occasionally at the present day as to 'adaptation.' The author admits that the piece is 'taken from the Greek.'

> 'non negat
> Personas transtulisse in Eunuchum suam
> Ex Græcâ, sed eas fabulas factas prius
> Latinas.'

Those curious on the subject as regards the English stage will do well to consult Mr. Collier's interesting work, 'The Annals of the Stage,' from the 3rd volume of which, p. 427, the following extract 'On the Payment of Actors' is taken:—

'The performers at our earlier theatres were distinguished into wholesharers, three-quarter sharers, half sharers, and hired men.' Into how many shares the receipts at the doors were divided in any instance does not appear, and doubtless it depended upon the number of persons of which a company consisted, and other circumstances. Malone (Shakspeare by Boswell, iii. 178) 'suspected' that the money taken was separated into forty portions, and that the receipts at the 'Globe' or 'Blackfriars' did not usually amount to more than 9l. on each performance. He assigns fifteen of the forty shares to the house-

---

[1] *Eunuchus.*   [2] Sat. vii. 87.

keepers or proprietors, and twenty-two shares to the actors, leaving three shares to be applied *to the purchase of new plays.* His notion of the nightly receipts was founded upon the accounts of Sir Henry Herbert, which on this point do not begin earlier than the year 1628. The king's players performing in the summer at the 'Globe' and in the winter at 'Blackfriars' allowed him a benefit at each theatre for five years and a half,' during which his receipts averaged 8*l*. 19*s*. 4*d*. Malone imagines that on remarkable occasions the receipts at the doors of the 'Globe' or 'Blackfriars' might amount to 20*l*. The author of 'The Actors' Remonstrance,' 1643, says that the 'housekeepers' shared ten, twenty, nay thirty shillings, which they put into 'their large and well-stuffed pockets.'

'Sharers, half sharers, and hired men are mentioned in the old satirical play, "Histriomastix," 1610. In one scene the dissolute performers, having been arrested by soldiers, one of the latter exclaims "Come on, players! Now we are sharers and you the hired men;" and in another scene, Clout, one of the characters, rejects with some indignation the offer of " half a share." In the same production we also meet with the term "master sharers." They are spoken of by an officer as more substantial men. . . . . Some of the actors or master-sharers were also proprietors of more shares than one. Gamaliel Ratsey, in that rare tract called "Ratsei's Ghost," printed about 1606, knights the principal performer of a company by the title of Sir Three-Shares-and-a-Half; and Tucca, in Ben Jonson's "Poetaster" (played in 1601), addressing Histrio, observes— "Commend me to Seven-Shares-and-a-half," as if some individual at that period had engrossed as large a proportion. Shakspeare, in "Hamlet," speaks of "a whole share" as a source of no contemptible emolument, and of the owner of it as a person filling no inferior station in "a cry of players." In "Northward Ho!" also a sharer is mentioned with respect. Bellamont, the poet, enters and tells his servant—

"Sirrah, I'll speak with none."

On which the servant asks—

"Not a player?"

And his master replies—

"No, though a sharer bawl;
I'll speak with none, although it be the mouth
Of the big company."

'Three-quarter sharers are mentioned in "The Ant and the Nightingale," 1604, where it is said "the Ant began to stalk later a three-quarter sharer." In the complaint against Henslowe drawn up by Joseph Taylor and other players in 1614 it is mentioned that some who had been only "three-quarter sharers" had advanced themselves to whole sharers.

'The value of a share in any particular company would depend upon the number of subdivisions, upon the popularity of the body, upon the stock plays belonging to it, upon the extent of its wardrobe, and the nature of its properties.'

The 'hired men' were paid like ordinary actors of the present day, by the week.

'Among the curious papers found by Malone at Dulwich College was one which throws light on the stipulations entered into by actors, on condition that they were allowed a share of the proceeds of the theatre. 'Henslowe and Meade having rebuilt Paris Garden in 1613, as a playhouse, and as a place where bears, &c., were to be baited, on the 7th April, 1614, entered into what are now technically called "articles" with Robert Dawes, to play there for three years, "for and at the rate of one whole share, according to the custom of players," and Dawes on his part covenanted to attend all rehearsals or forfeit twelve pence; to be ready dressed to begin the play at three in the afternoon, "unless by six of the company he shall be licensed to the contrary," or forfeit 3s.; if he "shall happen to be overcome with drink by the judgment of four of the company," when he ought to be fit to play, to forfeit 10s.; and if he fail to come to play, "having no licence or just excuse of sickness," to forfeit 20s. . . . .

'From the will of Thomas Pope, a celebrated actor, dated the 20th July, 1603,[1] we learn that he owned shares in two different and unconnected theatres at the same time, viz., the "Globe" and "Curtain," and perhaps played at both. . . . .

'Another source of emolument to performers of eminence, was the articling of apprentices, who were most likely engaged by the companies to which their masters belonged, and their earnings, or a portion of them, appropriated to those masters. . . .

'The performance of plays at Court, from a very early date seems to have been a considerable source of emolument to players. Prior to the reign of Elizabeth the rewards for such services varied considerably, but from the year 1562 to 1574 6l. 13s. 4d. were allowed for each play. After this date an addition of 3l. 6s. 8d., "by way of her Majesty's reward," was always made, so that the price of each play in London, by whatever company represented, was constantly 10l.'

Companies of players were also not unfrequently employed at marriages, christenings, and the like, the remuneration varying, no doubt, with the circumstances and disposition of the person at whose house they exhibited.

[1] Published by Chalmers, Supp. Apol. 162.

NOTE C. REMUNERATION OF AUTHORS.

'The custom of performers of dramatic representations journeying from place to place is very ancient, and frequent instances of the kind, particularly in the reign of Henry VI., are given in the "Annals of the Stage." Many noblemen at that date had companies of players as their retainers, and they, to use an expression of one of our old dramatists, " travelled upon the hard hoof from village to village," and from country seat to country seat, receiving uncertain rewards for their exhibitions.

'It does not seem to have been usual for chief actors of the established companies of London to travel into the country, unless the capital were at any period visited by the plague. In general only the inferior performers left the metropolis, and J. Stephens, giving the character of a "common player" observes, " I prefix the epithet of *common* to distinguish the base and artless appendants of our city companies, which oftentimes start away into rustical wanderings, and then like Proteus start back again into the city number."[1] . . . . The receipts in the country were always smaller than in London, and in several instances Henslowe stipulates with his hirelings that, should the company be obliged to go into the country, they should play "at half wages."'

'From 1660 to 1694,' says Dr. Reade, ("The Eighth Commandment," p. 274) 'authors in England were paid by the overplus of the third day. It seems to have averaged 100*l*., but before the close of the century Southerne demanded the overplus of the sixth night as well as the third, and obtained it. In 1705 a piece of Farquhar's having run the unparalleled number of fifty nights he obtained a third, viz., the ninth.'

'The following actual figures,' says Dr. Reade, 'are all I have been able to ascertain:—

'1688, when the author had only the third night's overplus, we learn from Downes, the prompter, that the " Squire of Alsatia" brought the author 130*l*., being the highest surplus recollected at single prices. They sometimes raised the prices for a new play.

'In 1694, under the two-night system, one of Southerne's nights brought him in 140*l*. The play was the "Fatal Marriage,' Mrs. Behn's story dramatised. Besides this market the dramatist was, since the war, allowed to sell his copyright to the booksellers.'

'Henslowe's Diary' contains 'very curious and conclusive information respecting the ordinary rewards of dramatists in his day. Those rewards seem to have varied sometimes according to circumstances, with which we are not acquainted. The highest price Henslowe appears, from this manuscript, ever to have given, was for "Page of Plymouth," by Ben

---

[1] *Essays and Characters*, 8vo. 1615.

Jonson and Dekker, a tragedy founded upon a murder committed by a wife in 1591. For this piece the old manager paid 11*l.* in August, 1599.... "Patient Grissell"[1] in December, 1599, cost him 9*l.* 10*s.* ... The sum generally paid for putting an old play on the stage, on its revival with such changes as seemed necessary, was 2*l.*, and this sum Edward Alleyn obtained for "Tambercam" and several others, but now and then the expense was considerably more, and Birds and Rowley had 4*l.* in November, 1602, for their "additions" to "Faustus."'

When a play became unusually popular, and therefore profitable, gratuities were now and then, though rarely, allowed to the authors by way of encouragement; thus Drayton, Wilson, Munday and Hathway received 10*s.* as a gift.

Notwithstanding the multiplicity of plays written for the association with which Henslowe was connected, it is quite clear from evidence supplied by the manuscript in our hands, as well as that obtained from other sources, that the wonderfully prolific dramatists of that day wrote for other companies also. They do not seem like Shakspeare to have confined themselves necessarily to one theatre, and to one body of actors. It is very possible that our great dramatist was under some express engagement not to compose any play for a rival company, and it is certain with regard to two of the popular authors in the pay of Henslowe that such was the case. On the 28th of February, 1698, Henry Porter undertook that Henslowe 'should have all the books which he wrote either himself or with any other,' and on the 25th of March, 1602, Henry Chettle sealed a bond with the Earl of Nottingham's players to write for them only. At these dates there existed a strong competition among different associations, but it must have been still stronger about ten or twelve years afterwards when Daborne was writing for Henslowe, when the price of new plays had risen considerably, and when he was threatening the old manager with carrying one of his productions to 'the king's men,' from whose service Shakspeare had very shortly before withdrawn, leaving the company in need of assistance. ... What connection this vast and rapid increase in the value of new plays may have had with the removal of Shakspeare from London we have no means of determining, but the fact deserves more notice than it has hitherto received.

---

[1] At p. 167 of this diary, as printed for the Shakspeare Society, is an item of 2*l.* paid to a printer, not named, as a gift to prevent the appearance of 'Patient Grissell' from the press, 'companies at that date holding it injurious to their interests that popular dramas should be made legible. This single fact (and the circumstance is nowhere else more distinctly stated) will explain how it happens that comparatively few old plays have been preserved.'—*Note*, Introd. xxv. *Hen. Dia.*

The contrast between the expenses of apparel and the cost of plays is remarkable. Heywood did not receive for the five admirable acts of his 'Woman Killed with Kindness' as much as was given by the company for the gown of the heroine.

In France the dramatist has now, for many years, been paid by a percentage on the gross receipts every night his play is performed; under the French system, a good first piece is worth from 1,500*l.* to 3,000*l.* Pousard received 4,000*l.* for 'La Bourse.' Dumas fils must have received 5,000*l.* for 'La Dame aux Camélias.'—*Reade*, p. 293.

That the system for remuneration of authors, as it now obtains, works sad injustice, now and then, in the case of those to whom the public owes its chief enjoyment is unfortunately but too true. One of the saddest instances, perhaps, is to be found in the history of the poet Cary, of whom Disraeli the elder, in his 'Curiosities of Literature,' writes: 'At this time, when the poet could neither walk the streets nor be seated at the convivial board without listening to his own songs and his own music—for, in truth, the whole nation was echoing his verse, and crowded theatres applauding his wit and humour—while this very man, urged by his strong humanity, founded a "Fund for Decayed Musicians," he was so broken-hearted, and his common comforts so utterly neglected, that, in despair, not waiting for nature to relieve him from the burden of existence, he laid violent hands upon himself, and when found dead had only a halfpenny in his pocket. Such was the fate of the author of some of the most popular pieces in our language . . .'

It was a case in which, however strong the right, adequate protection was by law impossible.

Note D.—'Caricature.'

The following extract from the *Daily Telegraph*, March 22, 1873, shows the curious relation that exists, in this respect, between the drama and the press:—

'Since the interference of the Lord Chamberlain with "The Happy Land," the obvious make-up of the three principal characters as cabinet ministers is of course at an end. Yet, although the dance has been prohibited, no power exists to prohibit a picture of it in which the "make-up" is faithfully preserved, and more than this, the owner of the picture not only finds his property so valuable, that it becomes worth his while to proceed against infringements upon his rights, but also is actually protected by the law. At the Guildhall, on Thursday, application was made under the sixth section of the Copyright Act (25 & 26 Vict. c. 68), on behalf of Messrs. Stannard & Son, publishers, for penalties for infringement of a lithograph, called "The Triumviri of the Happy Land. The celebrated make-up as prohibited by the Lord Chamberlain." It was stated that the Messrs. Stannard had published a representation of the scene enacted at the Court Theatre, in which the three principal characters were Mr. Gladstone, Mr. Lowe, and Mr. Ayrton, and that a certain Mr. Head, had thought proper to pirate the print in question and to sell copies of it at one penny each. The piracy it was argued was calculated to very much injure the sale of the original picture, and accordingly a summons was granted. It may seem at first a little strange that while the Lord Chamberlain was able to forbid the dance, the law not only allows a picture identical in spirit with the scene to be published, but actually protects the publisher against piracy. The explanation, however, is sufficiently easy. The objection to political allusions upon the stage, is based upon the very reasonable ground, that they are calculated to provoke riot and disturbance. A mere cartoon, however keen or broad its satire, has no such effect, and hence it is that "Punch" enjoys a liberty not conceded to a manager. Both the rule and its justification are so clear, that it is strange any misconception should ever have existed on the subject. It is an amusing instance of what has been called the "conflict of laws," that although Messrs. Righton, Fisher and Hill, are no longer allowed to "make up" as cabinet ministers, yet a picture faithfully representing them as so "made up," should be protected against piratical imitations.'

That courts were less sensitive in earlier times to criticisms administered from the stage, we may infer from the fact mentioned by Tytler, in his 'History of Scotland,' vol. iv. p. 255, that James V. and his Queen repeatedly witnessed the 'Morality,' I have above referred to (App. p. v.), in which the corruptions of the existing government and religion were treated with much severity.

As to libelling a person by signs, pictures and caricatures, see 'Starkie on Slander,' 3rd. Ed., p. 197.

NOTE E.—ENGLISH AND FRENCH AUTHORS.

WHETHER the intentions of the high contracting parties to this convention are not liable to be entirely defeated by the rather narrow doctrine as to alien authors prevalent in England (*Jeffreys* v. *Boosey*, 4 H. of L. Ca. 977. See, however, *Routledge* v. *Low*, L. R. 3 H. L. Ca. 100; 18 L. T. N.S. 874; 37 L. J. Ch. 454, per Westbury, C.), is a point very ably put by the writer of the following letter to the *Athenæum*, which appeared shortly after the conclusion of the treaty. The letter will be found reprinted 1 Jur. N.S. pt. ii. 523, Jan. 5, 1856:—

'Another flaw, it is believed, has been found in the Copyright Act. If our Courts of Law shall rule according to the letter of the International Convention—and we do not see how they can avoid such ruling—a mode of evasion has been discovered which will enable Americans, as well as all other aliens, to secure a copyright for works in this country. An experiment, having for its object to unsettle the law once more, is being made in the case of an Italian, Signor Ruffini, author of "Lorenzo Benoni" and "Doctor Antonio," two tales written in English and intended chiefly for circulation in England. Anticipating for "Doctor Antonio," which has just appeared, a popularity similar to that which attended "Lorenzo Benoni," Signor Ruffini's publishers, Messrs. Constable & Co., of Edinburgh, were led to look into the state of the law. They found, that though the English law alone offered no security, the French law of copyright, taken in connection with the International Copyright Convention between England and France, seemed to furnish it. Mr. Burke, in his "Analysis of the Copyright Laws," says, "According to the law of France, a French subject does not injure his copyright by publishing his work first in a foreign country. It matters not where that publication has taken place, the copyright forthwith accrues in France, and on the necessary deposit being effected, its infringement may be proceeded against in the French courts. Moreover, a foreigner publishing in France will enjoy the same copyright as a native, and this whether he has previously published *in his own or any other country or not*." Then comes the pleasantry. By the first article of the International Convention of 1852, it is provided that "the authors of works of literature and art, to whom the laws of either of the two countries do now, or may hereafter, give the right of property or copyright, shall be entitled to exercise that right in the territories of the other or such countries for the same term, and to the same extent, as the authors of works of the same nature, if published in such other country, would therein be entitled to exercise such right; so that the republication or piracy in either country of any work of literature or art published in the other, shall be dealt with in the same manner as the republication or piracy of a work of the same nature first published in the other country." Here the text is clear. Publication in France confers copyright in that country, and the holder of such copyright in France becomes, in virtue of the Convention of 1852, entitled to copyright in England! Let Signor Ruffini or Mr. Prescott first publish in Paris. He may then come to London and offer Mr. Murray or Mr. Bentley a monopoly of his works. Such, at least, is the new reading of the law which has been acted on in Signor Ruffini's case. His "Doctor Antonio" was published first in Paris, in English, by Galignani, all the formalities required by the French law being complied with, and thus it is supposed no copies of the work can be published in Great Britain except those issued by the Edinburgh publishers. Of course the Convention with France never contemplated the admission of Americans to its benefits, still an American holding a French copyright, which he can easily hold, becomes *quoad* copyright a Frenchman, and is entitled on the above interpretation to the protection of the Convention. Here is another and most powerful argument in favour of a revision of the law of copyright, as well as of the Convention to which it has given rise.'

Stage-right in France depends on the Law of the 19th January, 1791, the Law of the 6th August of the same year, the Imperial Decree of the 8th June, 1806, together with the published advice relative thereto of the Council of State of the 23rd August, 1811, the Law of the 3rd August, 1844, and the Penal Code, Art. 428.

The following is from the tabular form defining the nature and terms of duration of literary rights :—

Dramatic and Musical Copyright, which gives to Proprietor the right of representing or performing all species of Dramatic and Musical Pieces whatsoever.	For the life of the author, and for five years after his death for his heirs or assigns. In case, however, he leaves a widow or children, they will have, for twenty years after his death, the right of authorising the representation.

To secure the right, a copy of the play must be deposited at the Bibliothèque, and another at the office of the Minister of the Interior. An author does not, by French law, affect his right by prior publication out of France. Assignment should be in writing.—' Burke on International Copyright,' 46.

Piracy (*contrefaçon*) in France is, by Art. 425 of the Penal Code, declared criminal (*un délit*). Exposure for sale (*débit*) of pirated copies is (Art. 426) placed on the same footing as piratical publication. By Art. 427, the penalty for piracy is a fine not exceeding 100 frs., and for exposure for sale of pirated works a fine of from 25 frs. to 500 frs. with confiscation of pirated copies.

By Art. 428 of the Code : Every director, every proprietor of a theatre, every association of artists, who shall have caused to be represented on his or their stage dramatic works in contempt of the laws and regulations relative to copyright, will be punished by a fine of fifty francs at the least, of five hundred francs at the most, and the confiscation of the receipts.

Proceedings must be instituted within three years of the commission of the offence.

The author aggrieved may, at the same time that he prosecutes for the offence, obtain damages by civil suit. Deposit of the copy, wherever practicable, is a necessary condition precedent to any proceedings.

Note F.—Plagiarism.

'AMONG the most singular characters in literature, may be ranked those who do not blush to profess publicly the most dishonourable practices. The first vendor of printed sermons imitating manuscript, was, I think, Dr. Trusler. He to whom the following anecdotes relate, had superior ingenuity. Like the famous orator, Henley, he formed a school of his own. The present lecturer openly taught not to *imitate* the best authors, but to *steal* from them.'

'Richesource, a miserable declaimer, called himself "Moderator of the Academy of Philosophical Orators." He taught how a person destitute of literary talents might become eminent for literature, and published the principles of his art under the title of "The Mask of Orators or the Manner of disguising all kinds of composition, briefs, sermons, panegyrics, funeral orations, dedications, speeches, letters, passages, &c." I will give a notion of the work.

'The author very truly observes, that all who apply themselves to polite literature do not always find from their own funds a sufficient supply to ensure success. For such he labours and teaches to gather in the gardens of others those fruits of which their own sterile grounds are destitute; but so artfully to gather, that the public shall not perceive their depredations. He dignifies this fine art by the title of "Plagiarism," and thus explains it :—

'"The plagiarism of orators is the art, or an ingenious and easy mode which some adroitly employ to change or disguise all sorts of speeches of their own composition, or of that of other authors, for their pleasure or their utility in such a manner that it becomes impossible even for the author himself to recognise his own work, his own genius, and his own style, so skilfully shall the whole be disguised."

'Our professor proceeds to reveal the manner of managing the whole economy of the piece which is to be copied or disguised, and which consists in giving a new order to the parts, changing the phrases, the words, &c. An orator, for instance, having said that a plenipotentiary should possess three qualities—*probity*, *capacity*, and *courage*; the plagiarist, on the contrary, may employ *courage*, *capacity*, and *probity*. This is only for a general rule, for it is too simple to practise frequently. To render the part perfect we must render it more complex by changing the whole of the expressions. The plagiarist in place of *courage* will put *force*, *constancy*, or *vigour*. For *probity* he may say *religion*, *virtue*, or *sincerity*. Instead of *capacity* he may substitute *erudition*, *ability*, and *science*. Or he may disguise the whole by saying that the plenipotentiary should be firm, virtuous, and able.

'The rest of this uncommon work is composed of passages extracted from celebrated writers, which are turned into the new manner of the plagiarist. Their beauties, however, are never improved by their dress. Several celebrated writers when young, particularly the famous Fléchier, who addressed verses to him, frequented the lectures of the professor!

'Richesource became so zealous in this course of literature that he published a volume entitled "The Art of Writing and Speaking, or a Method of composing all sorts of Letters and holding a polite Conversation." He concludes his preface by advertising his readers that authors who may be in want of essays, sermons, letters of all kinds, written pleadings, and verses, may be accommodated on application to him.'—*Dis. Cur. Lit.* vol. ii. 219; 'Professors of Plagiarism and Obscurity.'

The reader may remember a famous scene in the 'Bourgeois Gentilhomme' of Molière, in which a similar feat is attempted, for the benefit of M. Jourdain, by the Professor.

In the 'Critic,' the last dramatic effort of Sheridan's genius, we have some admirable satire on this sad foible of authordom:

Sir Fretful Plagiary. I can tell you it is not always so safe to leave a play in the hands of those who write themselves.
Sneerwell. What! they may steal from them, my dear Plagiary?
Sir Fret. Steal! To be sure they may, and egad serve your best thoughts as gipsies do stolen children, disfigure them to make 'em pass for their own.
—[Act I. Sc. 1.]

Beefeater. Perdition seize my soul but I do love thee.
Sneerwell. Haven't I heard that line before?
Puff. No, I fancy not—Where?
Dangle. Yes, I think there is something like it in Othello.
Puff. Gad! Now you put me in mind on't, I believe there is—but that's of no consequence. All that can be said is that two people happened to hit on the same thought, and Shakspeare made use of it first, that's all.
—[Act. III. Sc. 3.]

The following remarks as to *translations* occur in Dryden's preface to Ovid's Epistles and Life of Lucian.

'All translations, I suppose, may be reduced to these three heads; first, that of metaphrase, or turning an author word for word, and line by line from one language into another. Thus or near this manner was " Horace—His Art of Poetry," translated by Ben Jonson. The second way is that of paraphrase or translation with latitude; where the author is kept in view by the translator, so as never to be lost; but his words are not so strictly followed as his sense, and that too is admitted to be amplified, but not altered. Such is Mr. Waller's translation of Virgil's fourth Æneid. The third way is that of imitation, where the translator (if now he has not lost that name) assumes the liberty, not only to vary from the words and sense, but to forsake them both, as he sees occasion, and taking only some general limits from the original to run divisions on the groundwork as he pleases. Such is Mr. Cowley's practice in turning two odes of Pindar, and one of Horace, into English.'—Dryden's Works, Scott's ed. xx. 11.

'A translator that would write with any force or spirit of an original, must never dwell on the words of his author. He ought to possess himself entirely, and perfectly comprehend the genius and sense, of his author, the nature of the subject, and the terms of the act or subject treated of, and then he will express himself as justly and with as much life, as if he wrote an original.' Ib. xviii. 81.

Statutes

relating to Stage-right, Dramatic Copyright, Lectures, and the Regulation of Theatres.

I. Statute 3 & 4 Will. IV. c. 15.

An Act to amend the Laws relating to Dramatic Literary Property.

[10 June 1833.]

<small>54 Geo. III. 156.</small>

1. Whereas by an Act passed in the fifth-fourth year of the reign of his late Majesty King George the Third, intituled ' An Act to amend the several Acts for the Encouragement of Learning by securing the Copies and Copyright of Printed Books to the Authors of such books or their Assigns,' it was amongst other things provided and enacted, that from and after the passing of the said Act, the author of any book or books composed, and not printed or published, or which should thereafter be composed and printed and published, and his assignee or assignees, should have the sole liberty of printing and reprinting such book or books for the full term of twenty-eight years, to commence from the day of first publishing the same, and also, if the author should be living at the end of that period, for the residue of his natural life; and whereas it is expedient to extend the provisions of the said Act, be it therefore enacted by the King's most excellent Majesty, by and with the advice and consent of the Lords spiritual and temporal and Commons in this present Parliament assembled, and by the authority of the same, that from and after the passing of this Act the author of any tragedy, comedy, play, opera, farce, or any other dramatic piece or entertainment composed and not printed and published by the author thereof or his assignee, or which (hereafter) (shall) be composed and not printed or published by the author thereof or his assignee, or the assignee of such author shall have as his own property the sole liberty of representing or

<small>The author of any dramatic piece shall have as his property the sole liberty of representing it or causing it to be represented at any place of dramatic entertainment.</small>

causing to be represented at any place or places of dramatic entertainment whatsoever in any part of the United Kingdom of Great Britain and Ireland, in the Isles of Man, Jersey and Guernsey, or in any part of the British dominions, any such production as aforesaid, not printed and published by the author thereof or his assignee, and shall be deemed and taken to be the proprietor thereof; and that the author of any such production printed and published within ten years before the passing of this Act by the author thereof or his assignee, or which shall hereafter be so printed and published, or the assignee of such author shall from the time of passing this Act, or from the time of such publication respectively, until the end of twenty-eight years from the day of such first publication of the same, and also if the author or authors or the survivor of the authors shall be living at the end of that period, during the residue of his natural life, have as his own property the sole liberty of representing, or causing to be represented, the same at any such place of dramatic entertainment as aforesaid, and shall be deemed and taken to be the proprietor thereof, provided, nevertheless, that nothing in this Act contained shall prejudice, alter or affect the right or authority of any person to represent or cause to be represented, at any place or places of dramatic entertainment whatsoever, any such production as aforesaid, in all cases in which the author thereof or his assignee shall, previously to the passing of this Act, have given his consent to or authorised such representation, but that such sole liberty of the author or his assignee shall be subject to such right or authority.

Proviso as to cases when previous to the passing of this Act a consent has been given.

2. And be it further enacted, that if any person shall during the continuance of such sole liberty as aforesaid, contrary to the intent of this Act, or right of the author or his assignee, represent or cause to be represented, without the consent in writing of the author or other proprietor first had and obtained, at any place of dramatic entertainment within the limits aforesaid, any such production as aforesaid, or any part thereof, every such offender shall be liable for each and every such representation to the payment of an amount not less than forty shillings, or to the full amount of the benefit or advantage arising from such representation, or the injury or loss sustained by the plaintiff therefrom whichever shall be the greater damages to the author or other proprietor of such production so represented, contrary to the true intent and meaning of this Act, to be recovered, together with double costs of suit, by such author or other proprietor in any Court having jurisdiction in such cases in that part of the said United Kingdom or of the British dominions in which the offence shall be committed, and in every such proceeding where the sole liberty of such author or his assignee as afore-

Penalty on performing pieces contrary to this Act.

said shall be subject to such right or authority as aforesaid, it shall be sufficient for the plaintiff to state that he has such sole liberty without stating the same to be subject to such right or authority or otherwise mentioning the same.

Limitation of actions.

3. Provided, nevertheless, and be it further enacted that all actions or proceedings for any offence or injury that shall be committed against this Act, shall be brought, sued and commenced within twelve calendar months next after such offence committed, or else the same shall be void and of no effect.

Explanation of words.

4. And be it further enacted, that whenever authors, persons, offenders or others are spoken of in this Act in the singular number or in the masculine gender, the same shall extend to any number of persons and to either sex.

II. Statute 5 & 6 Will. IV. c. 65.

An Act for preventing the publication of Lectures without Consent.

[9th September 1835.]

1. Whereas printers, publishers and other persons have frequently taken the liberty of printing and publishing lectures delivered upon divers subjects, without the consent of the authors of such lectures, or the persons delivering the same in public, to the great detriment of such authors and lecturers,

Authors of lectures, or their assigns, to have the sole right of publishing them.

be it enacted, &c., that from and after the first day of September, one thousand eight hundred and thirty-five, the author of any lecture or lectures, or the person to whom he hath sold or otherwise conveyed the copy thereof, in order to deliver the same in any school, seminary, institution or other place, or for any other purpose, shall have the sole right and liberty of printing and publishing such lecture or lectures; and that if

Penalty on other persons publishing lectures without leave.

any person shall by taking down the same in short-hand or otherwise in writing, or in any other way obtain or make a copy of such lecture or lectures, and shall print, or lithograph or otherwise copy and publish the same, or cause the same to be printed, lithographed or otherwise copied and published without leave of the author thereof, or of the person to whom the author thereof hath sold or otherwise conveyed the same, and every person who, knowing the same to have been printed or copied and published without such consent, shall sell, publish or expose to sale or cause to be sold, published, or exposed to sale any such lecture or lectures, shall forfeit such printed or otherwise copied lecture or lectures, or parts thereof, together with one penny for every sheet thereof which shall be found in his custody, either printed, lithographed or copied, or printing, lithographing or copying, published or exposed to sale, contrary to the true intent and meaning of this Act, the one moiety thereof to his Majesty, his heirs or successors, and the other moiety thereof to any person who shall sue for the same to be recovered in any of his Majesty's Courts of Record in Westminster, by action of debt, bill, plaint or information, in which no wager of law, essoign, privilege or protection, or more than one imparlance shall be allowed.

2. That any printer or publisher of any newspaper who shall, without such leave as aforesaid, print and publish in such newspaper any lecture or lectures shall be deemed and taken to be a person printing and publishing without leave within the provisions of this Act, and liable to the aforesaid forfeitures and penalties in respect of such printing and publishing. *Penalty on printers or publishers of newspapers publishing lectures without leave.*

3. That no person, allowed for certain fee and reward, or otherwise, to attend and be present at any lectures delivered in any place, shall be deemed and taken to be licensed, or to have leave to print, copy and publish such lectures only because of having leave to attend such lecture or lectures. *Persons having leave to attend lectures not on that account licensed to publish them.*

4. Provided always that nothing in this Act shall extend to prohibit any person from printing, copying and publishing any lecture or lectures which have or shall have been printed and published with leave of the authors thereof or their assignees, and whereof the time hath or shall have expired within which the sole right to print and publish the same is given by an Act passed in the eighth year of the reign of Queen Anne, intituled, 'An Act for the Encouragement of Learning by vesting the Copies of Printed Books in the Authors or Purchasers of such Copies during the Times therein mentioned,' and by another Act passed in the fifty-fourth year of the reign of King George the Third, intituled, 'An Act to amend the several Acts for the Encouragement of Learning, by securing the Copies and Copyright of Printed Books to the Authors of such books or their Assigns, or to any Lectures which have been printed or published before the passing of this Act.' *Act not to prohibit the publishing of lectures after expiration of the copyright. 8 Anne, c. 19. 54 Geo. III. c. 156.*

5. Provided further, that nothing in this Act shall extend to any lecture or lectures, or the printing, copying or publishing any lecture or lectures or parts thereof, of the delivering of which notice in writing shall not have been given to two justices living within five miles from the place where such lecture or lectures shall be delivered two days at the least before delivering the same, or to any lecture or lectures delivered in any University, or public school or college, or on any public foundation, or by any individual in virtue of or according to any gift, endowment or foundation, and that the law relating thereto shall remain the same as if this Act had not been passed. *Act not to extend to lectures delivered in unlicensed places, &c.*

III. Statute 5 & 6 Vic. c. 45.

An Act to Amend the Law of Copyright.

[1 July 1842.]

1. Whereas it is expedient to amend the Law relating to copyright, and to afford greater encouragement to the production of literary works of lasting benefit to the world, be it enacted, &c., that from the passing of this Act, an Act passed in the eighth year of her Majesty Queen Anne (8 *Anne*, c. 19), intituled 'An Act for the Encouragement of Learning by vesting the Copies of Printed Books in the Authors or Purchasers of such Copies during the Times therein mentioned,' and also an Act passed in the forty-first year of the reign of his Majesty King George the Third (41 *Geo.* III. c. 107), intituled 'An Act for the further Encouragement of Learning in the United Kingdom of Great Britain and Ireland, by securing the Copies and Copyright of Printed Books to the Authors of such books or their Assigns for the Time therein mentioned,' and also an Act passed in the fifty-fourth year of the reign of his Majesty King George the Third (54 *Geo.* III. c. 156), intituled 'An Act to amend the several Acts for the Encouragement of Learning, by securing the Copies and Copyright of Printed Books to the Authors of such books or their Assigns,' be and the same are hereby repealed, except so far as the continuance of either of them may be necessary for carrying on or giving effect to any proceedings at law or in equity pending at the time of passing this Act, or for enforcing any cause of action or suit, or any right or contract then subsisting.

Interpretation of Act.

2. And be it enacted, that in the construction of this Act, the word 'book' shall be construed to mean and include every volume, part or division of a volume, pamphlet, sheet of letter-press, sheet of music, map, chart, or plan separately published; that the words, 'dramatic piece,' shall be construed to mean and include every tragedy, comedy, play, opera, farce, or other scenic, musical, or dramatic entertainment; that the word 'copyright' shall be construed to mean the sole and exclusive liberty of printing or otherwise multiplying copies of any subject to which the said word is herein applied; that the words, *Personal representatives.* 'personal representative,' shall be construed to mean and include every executor, administrator, and next-of-kin entitled to administration; that the word *Assigns.* 'assigns' shall be construed to mean and include every person in whom the interest of an author in copyright shall be vested, whether derived from such author before or after the publication of any book, and whether

acquired by sale, gift, bequest, or by operation of law or otherwise ; that the words, 'British Dominions,' shall be construed to mean and include all parts of the United Kingdom of Great Britain and Ireland, the Islands of Jersey and Guernsey, all parts of the East and West Indies, and all the Colonies, settlements, and possessions of the Crown which now are or hereafter may be acquired ; and that whenever in this Act in describing any person, matter, or thing, the word importing the singular number or the masculine gender only is used, the same shall be understood to include and to be applied to several persons as well as one person, and females as well as males, and several matters or things as well as one matter or thing respectively, unless there shall be something in the subject or context repugnant to such construction.

3. And be it enacted, that the copyright in every book which shall, after the passing of this Act, be published in the lifetime of its author, shall endure for the natural life of such author, and for the further term of seven years commencing at the time of his death, and shall be the property of such author and his assigns; provided always that if the said term of seven years shall expire before the end of forty-two years from the first publication of such book, the copyright shall in that case endure for such period of forty-two years, and that the copyright in every book which shall be published after the death of its author, shall endure for the term of forty-two years from the first publication thereof, and shall be the property of the proprietor of the author's manuscript from which such book shall be first published, and his assigns. *Endurance of term of copyright in any book hereafter to be published in the lifetime of the author. If published after the author's death.*

4. And whereas it is just to extend the benefits of this Act to authors of books published before the passing thereof, and in which copyright still subsists, be it enacted that the copyright which at the time of passing this Act shall subsist in any book theretofore published (except as hereinafter mentioned), shall be extended and endure for the full term provided by this Act in cases of books thereafter published, and shall be the property of the person who at the time of passing of this Act shall be the proprietor of such copyright. Provided always, that in all cases in which such copyright shall belong in whole or in part to a publisher, or other person who shall have acquired it for other consideration than that of natural love and affection, such copyright shall not be extended by this Act, but shall endure for the term which shall subsist therein at the time of passing of this Act and no longer, unless the author of such book, if he shall be living, or the personal representative of such author, if he shall be dead, and the proprietor of such copyright, shall before the expiration of such term consent and agree to accept the benefits of this Act in respect of such book, and shall cause a minute of such consent, in the form in *In cases of subsisting copyright the term to be extended except when it shall belong to an assignee for other consideration than natural love and affection in which case it shall cease at the expiration of the present term, unless an extension be agreed between the proprietor and the author.*

that behalf given in the schedule to this Act annexed, to be entered in the book of registry hereinafter directed to be kept, in which case such copyright shall endure for the full term by this Act provided in cases of books to be published after the passing of this Act, and shall be the property of such person or persons as in such minute shall be expressed.

5. [*Judicial Committee of the Privy Council may license the republication of books which the proprietor refuses to republish after the death of the author.*]

6. [*Copies of books published after the passing of the Act, and of all subsequent editions, to be delivered within certain times at the British Museum.*]

7. [*Mode of delivering at the British Museum.*]

8. [*A copy of every book to be delivered within a month after demand to the officer of the Stationers' Company for the following libraries—the Bodleian at Oxford, the Public Library at Cambridge, the Faculty of Advocates at Edinburgh, and that of Trinity College, Dublin.*]

9. [*Publishers may deliver copies to the Libraries instead of at Stationers' Company.*]

10. [*Penalty for default in delivering copies for the use of the Libraries.*]

<small>Book of registry to be kept at Stationers' Hall.</small>

11. And be it enacted that a book of Registry wherein may be registered, as hereinafter enacted, the proprietorship in the copyright of books and assignments thereof, and in dramatic and musical pieces, whether in manuscript or otherwise, and licences affecting such copyrights, shall be kept at the Hall of the Stationers' Company, by the officer appointed by the said company for the purposes of this Act; and shall at all convenient times be open to the inspection of any person on payment of one shilling for every entry which shall be searched for or inspected in the said book, and that such officers shall, whenever thereunto reasonably required, give a copy of any entry in such book, certified under his hand and impressed with the stamp of the said company to be provided by them for that purpose, and which they are hereby required to provide to any person requiring the same on payment to him of the sum of five shillings, and such copies so certified and impressed shall be received in evidence in all Courts, and in all summary proceedings, and shall be *primâ facie* proof of the proprietorship or assignment of copyright or licence as therein expressed, but subject to be rebutted by other evidence; and in the case of dramatic or musical pieces, shall be *primâ facie* proof of the right of representation or performance, subject to be rebutted as aforesaid.

<small>Inspection.</small>

<small>Copy of entry.</small>

<small>Copy to be evidence.</small>

<small>Making a false entry, or producing false copy a</small>

12. And be it enacted, that if any person shall wilfully make, or cause to be made, any false entry in the Registry Book of the Stationers' Company, or shall wilfully produce or cause to

be tendered in evidence, any paper falsely purporting to be a copy of any entry in the said book, he shall be guilty of an indictable misdemeanour, and shall be punished accordingly. *[misdemeanour.]*

13. And be it enacted, that after the passing of this Act it shall be lawful for the proprietor of copyright in any book heretofore published, or in any book hereafter to be published to make entry in the Registry book of the Stationers' Company of the title of such book, the time of the first publication thereof, the name and place of abode of the publisher thereof and the name and place of abode of the proprietor of the copyright of the said book, or of any portion of such copyright in the form in that behalf given in the schedule to this Act annexed upon payment of the sum of five shillings to the officer of the said Company, and that it shall be lawful for every such registered proprietor to assign his interest or any portion of his interest therein, by making entry in the said book of registry of such assignment, and of the name and place of abode of the assignee thereof in the form given in that behalf in the said schedule on payment of the like sum, and such assignment so entered shall be effectual in law to all intents and purposes whatsoever, without being subject to any stamp or duty, and shall be of the same force and effect as if such assignment had been made by deed. *[Entries of copyright may be used in the book of registry]*

14. And be it enacted, that if any person shall deem himself aggrieved by any entry made under colour of this Act in the said book of registry, it shall be lawful for such person to apply by motion to the Court of Queen's Bench, Court of Common Pleas, or Court of Exchequer in term time, or to apply by summons to any judge of either of such Courts in vacation, for an order that such entry may be expunged or varied, and that upon any such application by motion or summons to either of the said Courts or to a judge as aforesaid, such court or judge shall make such order for expunging, varying or confirming such entry either with or without costs as to such Court or judge shall seem just, and the officer appointed by the Stationers' Company, for the purposes of this Act, shall on the production to him of any such order for expunging or varying any such entry, expunge or vary the same according to the requisitions of such order. *[Persons aggrieved by entry in registry may apply to a Court of Law in term or Judge in vacation who may order entry to be varied or expunged.]*

15. And be it enacted, that if any person shall in any part of the British dominions after the passing of this Act print, or cause to be printed, either for sale or exportation, any book in which there shall be subsisting copyright, without the consent in writing of the proprietor thereof, or shall import for sale or hire any such book so having been unlawfully printed from parts beyond the sea, or knowing such book to have been so unlawfully printed or imported, shall sell, publish, or expose to sale, or hire or cause to be sold, published, or exposed to sale or hire, *[Remedy for piracy by action on the case.]*

or shall have in his possession for sale or hire, any such book so unlawfully printed or imported without such consent as aforesaid, such offender shall be liable to a special action on the case at the suit of the proprietor of such copyright to be brought in any Court of Record in that part of the British dominions in which the offence shall be committed, provided always that in Scotland such offender shall be liable to an action in the Court of Session in Scotland, which shall and may be brought and prosecuted in the same manner in which any other action of damages to the like amount may be brought and prosecuted there.

<small>In actions for piracy defendant to give notice of objections to the plaintiff's title on which he means to rely.</small>

16. And be it enacted, that after the passing of this Act in any action brought within the British dominions against any person for printing any such book for sale, hire, or exportation, or for importing, selling, publishing, or exposing to sale or hire, or causing to be imported, sold, published, or exposed to sale or hire, any such book, the defendant on pleading thereto shall give to the plaintiff a notice in writing of any objections on which he means to rely on the trial of such action, and if the nature of his defence be that the plaintiff in such action was not the author or first publisher of the book in which he shall by such action claim copyright, or is not the proprietor of the copyright therein, or that some other person than the plaintiff was the author or first publisher of such book, or is the proprietor of the copyright therein, then the defendant shall specify in such notice the name of the person who he alleges to have been the author or first publisher of such book, or the proprietor of the copyright therein, together with the title of such book, and the time when, and the place where such book was first published, otherwise the defendant in such action shall not at the trial or hearing of such action, be allowed to give any evidence that the plaintiff in such action was not the author or first publisher of the book in which he claims such copyright as aforesaid, or that he was not the proprietor of the copyright therein, and at such trial or hearing no other objection shall be allowed to be made on behalf of such defendant than the objections stated in such notice, or that any other person was the author or first publisher of such book or the proprietor of the copyright therein, than the person specified in such notice, or give in evidence in support of his defence any other book than one substantially corresponding in title, time and place of publication with the title, time and place specified in such notice.

17. [*No person except the proprietor, &c., shall import for sale or hire, copies piractically printed abroad of any book first composed &c. within the United Kingdom, and reprinted elsewhere under penalty of forfeiture and of* 10l., *and double value. Books may be seized by officers of Customs or Excise.*]

18. [*As to copyright in encyclopædias, periodicals, and works published in a series, reviews or magazines. Proviso for authors who have reserved the right of publishing their articles in a separate form.*]

19. [*Proprietors of encyclopædias, periodicals, and works published in series, may enter at once at Stationers' Hall and thereon have the benefit of the registration of the whole.*]

20. 'And whereas an Act was passed in the third year of the reign of his late Majesty to amend the law relating to dramatic literary property, and it is expedient to extend the term of the sole liberty of representing dramatic pieces given by that Act to the full time by this Act provided for the continuance of copyright, and whereas it is expedient to extend to musical compositions the benefits of that Act, and also of this Act,' be it therefore enacted, that the provisions of the said Act of his late Majesty, and of this Act shall apply to musical compositions, and that the sole liberty of representing or performing or causing or permitting to be represented or performed, any dramatic piece or musical composition, shall endure and be the property of the author thereof and his assigns for the term in this Act provided for the duration of copyright in books; and the provisions hereinbefore enacted in respect of the property of such copyright and of registering the same, shall apply to the liberty of representing or performing any dramatic piece or musical composition as if the same were herein expressly reenacted and applied thereto, save and except that the first public representation or performance of any dramatic piece or musical composition, shall be deemed equivalent in the construction of this Act to the first publication of any book, provided always that in case of any dramatic piece or musical composition in manuscript, it shall be sufficient for the person having the sole liberty of representing or performing, or causing to be represented or performed, the same to register only the title thereof, the name and place of abode of the author or composer thereof, the name and place of abode of the proprietor thereof, and the time and place of its first representation or performance.

The provisions of 3 & 4 Will. IV. c. 15 extended to musical compositions and the term of copyright as provided by this Act applied to the liberty of representing dramatic pieces and musical compositions.

21. And be it enacted, that the person who shall at any time have the sole liberty of representing such dramatic piece or musical composition, shall have and enjoy the remedies given and provided in the said Act of the third and fourth years of the reign of his late Majesty, King William the Fourth, passed to amend the laws relating to dramatic literary property during the whole of his interest therein as fully as if the same were re-enacted in this Act.

Proprietors of right of dramatic representations shall have all the remedies given by 3 & 4 Will. IV. c. 15

22. And be it enacted, that no assignment of the copyright of any book consisting of, or containing a dramatic piece or musical composition shall be holden to convey to the assignee

Assignment of copyright of a dramatic piece not

to convey the right of representation.

the right of representing or performing such dramatic piece or musical composition, unless an entry in the said registry book shall be made of such assignment wherein shall be expressed the intention of the parties that such right should pass by such assignment.

23. [*Books pirated to be the property of proprietor of copyright and recoverable by action.*]

No proprietor of copyright commencing after this Act shall sue or proceed for any infringement before making entry in the book of registry.

24. And be it enacted, that no proprietor of copyright in any book which shall be first published after the passing of this Act, shall maintain any action or suit at law or in equity, or any summary proceeding in respect of any infringement of such copyright, unless he shall before commencing such action, suit or proceeding, have caused an entry to be made in the book of registry of the Stationers' Company of such book pursuant to this Act; Provided always that the omission to make such entry, shall not affect the copyright in any book, but only the right to sue or proceed in respect of the infringement thereof as aforesaid.

Proviso for dramatic pieces.

Provided also that nothing herein contained, shall prejudice the remedies which the proprietor of the sole liberty of representing any dramatic piece, shall have by virtue of the Act passed in the third year of the reign of his late Majesty, King William the Fourth to amend the laws relating to dramatic literary property or of this Act, although no entry shall be made in the book of registry aforesaid.

Copyright shall be personal property.

25. And be it enacted, that all copyright shall be deemed personal property, and shall be transmissible by bequest, or in case of intestacy, shall be subject to the same law of distribution as other personal property, and in Scotland shall be deemed to be personal and moveable estate.

General issue in certain actions.

26. And be it enacted, that if any action or suit shall be commenced or brought against any person or persons whomsoever for doing or causing to be done anything in pursuance of this Act, the defendant or defendants in such action may plead the general issue, and give the special matter in evidence;

Costs.

and if upon such action a verdict shall be given for the defendant, or the plaintiff shall become nonsuited or discontinue his action, then the defendant shall have and recover his full costs, for which he shall have the same remedy as a defendant in any case by law hath.

Limitation of actions.

And that all actions, suits, bills, indictments, or informations for any offence that shall be committed against this Act, shall be brought, sued, and commenced within twelve calendar months next after such offence committed, or else the same shall be void and of none effect.

Not to extend to actions, &c., in respect to delivery of book.

Provided that such limitation of time shall not extend or be construed to extend to any actions, suits, or other proceedings which, under the authority of this Act, shall or may be brought, sued, or commenced for or in respect of any copies of books to be delivered for the use of the British Museum, or of any one of the four libraries hereinbefore mentioned.

27. [*Saving the rights of the Universities and Colleges of Eton, Westminster, and Winchester.*]

28. [*Saving all subsisting rights, contracts, and engagements.*] <small>Extent of the Act.</small>

29. That this Act shall extend to the United Kingdom of Great Britain and Ireland, and to every part of the British dominions.

SCHEDULE to which the preceding Act refers.

No. 1. FORM OF MINUTE OF CONSENT TO BE ENTERED AT STATIONERS' HALL.

We, the undersigned, A. B., of   , the author of a certain book, entitled Y. Z. [or the personal representative of the author, *as the case may be*] and C. D., of   , do hereby certify that we have consented and agreed to accept the benefits of the Act passed in the fifth year of the reign of her Majesty Queen Victoria, cap. 45, for the extension of the term of copyright therein provided by the said Act, and hereby declare that such extended term of copyright therein is the property of the said A. B. [*or* C. D.]

Dated this   day of   , 18 .

(Signed)   A. B.
           C. D.

Witness

To the Registering Officer appointed by the Stationers' Company.

[Her Majesty's reign commenced on the 20th June, 1837, and her royal assent was given to this Act on the 1st July, 1842; consequently, the Act was passed in the sixth year of the Queen, and should be so pleaded, or as having been passed 'in the session held in the fifth and sixth year of her Majesty Queen Victoria,' *Rex* v. *Biers*, 3 N. & M. 475; *Gibbs* v. *Pike*, 8 Mee. & W. 223. The schedule was drawn in the fifth year of the Queen, and has not been corrected. It will be advisable in the minute of consent, to state the year by a reference to the session which will include the words of the schedule.—Sweet's note to Jarm. & Byth., vol. vii., p. 618.]

No. 2. FORM OF REQUIRING ENTRY OF PROPRIETORSHIP.

I, A. B., of   , do hereby certify that I am the proprietor of the copyright of a book entitled Y. Z., and I hereby require you to make entry in the register book of the Stationers' Company of my proprietorship of such copyright, according to the particulars underwritten.

Title of book.	Name of publisher and place of publication.	Name and place of abode of the proprietor of the copyright.	Date of first publication.
Y. Z.		A. B.	

Dated this   day of   , 18 .
Witness   C. D.   (Signed) A. B.

No. 3. ORIGINAL ENTRY OF PROPRIETORSHIP OF COPYRIGHT OF A BOOK.

Time of making the entry.	Title of book.	Name of the publisher and place of publication.	Name and place of abode of the proprietor of the copyright.	Date of first publication.
	Y. Z.	A. B.	C. D.	

No. 4. FORM OF CONCURRENCE OF THE PARTY ASSIGNING * IN ANY BOOK PREVIOUSLY REGISTERED.

I, A. B., of   , being the assigner of the copyright of the book hereunder described, do hereby require you to make entry of the assignment of the copyright therein.

Title of book.	Assigner of the copyright.	Assignee of the copyright.
Y. Z.	A. B.	C. D.

Dated this   day of   , 18 .
                         (Signed) A. B.

* The words, 'his interest,' are here omitted.—Sweet.

No. 5.   Form of Entry of Assignment of Copyright in any Book previously Registered.

Date of entry.	Title of book.	Assigner of copyright.	Assignee of copyright.
	Set out the title of the book, and refer to the page of the registry book in which the original entry of the copyright thereof is made.	A. B.	C. D. * [This should contain the name and *place of abode* of the assignee, see § 13.]

IV.   Statute 6 & 7 Vic. c. 68.

An Act for Regulating Theatres.

[22 August 1843.]

1. Whereas it is expedient that the laws now in force for regulating theatres and theatrical performances be repealed and other provisions be enacted in their stead, Be it enacted, &c., that an Act passed in the third year of the reign of King James the First intituled, 'An Act to restrain the Abuses of Players' (3 Jas. I. c. 21), and so much of an Act passed in the tenth year of the reign of King George the Second (10 Geo. II. 19), for the more effectual preventing the unlawful playing of interludes within the precincts of the two universities— that part of Great Britain called England and the places adjacent as is now in force, and another Act passed in the tenth year of the reign of King George the Second, intituled, 'An Act to explain and amend so much of an Act made in the twelfth year of the reign of Queen Anne (*ante* p. 36, *n.*) intituled, "An Act for reducing the Laws relating to Rogues, Vagabonds, Sturdy Beggars, and Vagrants into one Act of Parliament, and for the more effectual punishing such Rogues, Vagabonds, Sturdy Beggars, and Vagrants and sending them whither they ought to be sent," as relates to common players of interludes' (10 Geo. II. c. 28), and another Act passed in the twenty-eighth year of the reign of King George the Third intituled, 'An Act to enable Justices of the Peace to license theatrical representations occasionally under the restrictions therein contained,' shall be repealed.

(Proviso saving the Licenses then in force.)

<small>All theatres for the performance of plays must be licensed.</small>

2. And be it enacted that, except as aforesaid, it shall not be lawful for any person to have or keep any house or other place of public resort in Great Britain for the public performance of stage plays without authority by virtue of letters patent from her Majesty, her heirs and successors or predecessors, or without license from the Lord Chamberlain of her Majesty's household for the time being, or from the justices of the peace, as hereinafter provided; and every person who shall offend against this enactment shall be liable to forfeit such sum as shall be awarded by the Court in which or the justices by whom he shall be convicted, not exceeding twenty pounds for every day on which such house or place shall have been so kept open by him for the purpose aforesaid without legal authority.

<small>What licences shall be granted by the Lord Chamberlain.</small>

3. And be it enacted, that the authority of the Lord Chamberlain for granting licences shall extend to all theatres (not being Patent Theatres) within the parliamentary boundaries of the cities of London and Westminster, and of the boroughs of Finsbury and Marylebone, the Tower Hamlets, Lambeth, and Southwark, and also within those places where her Majesty, her heirs and successors, shall in their royal persons occasionally reside: Provided always, that except within the cities and boroughs aforesaid and the boroughs of New Windsor in the county of Berks, and Brighthelmstone in the county of Sussex, licences for theatres may be granted by the justices as hereinafter provided in those places in which her Majesty, her heirs and successors, shall occasionally reside; but such licences shall not be in force during the residence there of her Majesty, her heirs and successors, and during such residence it shall not be lawful to open such theatres as last aforesaid (not being Patent Theatres) without the licence of the Lord Chamberlain.

<small>Fee for Lord Chamberlain's licence.</small>

4. And be it enacted, that for every such licence granted by the Lord Chamberlain, a fee not exceeding ten shillings for each calendar month during which the theatre is licensed to be kept open according to such scale of fees as shall be fixed by the Lord Chamberlain, shall be paid to the Lord Chamberlain.

<small>Licences may be granted by Justices.</small>

5. And be it enacted, that the Justices of the Peace, within every county, riding, division, liberty, cinque port, city, and borough in Great Britain beyond the limits of the authority of the Lord Chamberlain in which application shall have been made to them for any such licence as is hereinafter mentioned, shall, within twenty-one days next after such application shall have been made to them in writing, signed by the party making

the same and countersigned by at least two justices acting in and for the division within which the property proposed to be licensed shall be situate, and delivered to the clerk to the said justices, hold a special Session in the division, district, or place for which they usually act for granting licences to houses for the performance of stage-plays, of the holding of which session seven days' notice shall be given by their clerk to each of the justices acting within such division, district, or place; and every such licence shall be given under the hands and seals of four or more of the justices assembled at such special Session, and shall be signed and sealed in open Court, and afterwards shall be publicly read by the clerk with the names of the justices subscribing the same.

6. And be it enacted that, for every such licence granted by the justices, a fee not exceeding five shillings for each calendar month during which the theatre is licensed to be kept open according to such scale of fees as shall be fixed by the justices shall be paid to the clerk of the said justices. Fees for Justice's licence.

7. And be it enacted, that no such licence for a theatre shall be granted by the Lord Chamberlain or justices to any person except the actual and responsible manager for the time being of the theatre in respect of which the licence shall be granted, and the name and place of abode of such manager shall be printed on every play bill announcing any representation at such theatre, and such manager shall become bound himself in such penal sum as the Lord Chamberlain or justices shall require, being in no case more than five hundred pounds, and two sufficient sureties to be approved by the said Lord Chamberlain or justices, each in such penal sum as the Lord Chamberlain or justices shall require, being in no case more than one hundred pounds, for the due observance of the rules which shall be in force at any time during the currency of the licence for the regulation of such theatre, and for securing payment of the penalties which such manager may be adjudged to pay for breach of the said rules, or any of the provisions of this Act. To whom licences shall be granted.

8. And be it enacted, that in case it shall appear to the Lord Chamberlain that any riot or misbehaviour has taken place in any theatre licensed by him or in any Patent Theatre, it shall be lawful for him to suspend such licence or to order such Patent Theatre to be closed for such time as to him shall seem fit, and it shall also be lawful for the Lord Chamberlain to order that any Patent Theatre or any theatre licensed by him shall be closed on such public occasions as to the Lord Chamberlain shall seem fit, and while any such licence shall be suspended or any such order shall be in force the theatre to which the same applies shall not be entitled to the privilege of any letters patent or licence, but shall be deemed an unlicensed house. Rules for the Theatres under the control of the Lord Chamberlain.

xxxvi APPENDIX.

Rules for enforcing order in the theatres licensed by Justices.

9. And be it enacted, that the said justices of the peace, at a special licensing session, or at some adjournment thereof, shall make suitable rules for ensuring order and decency at the several theatres licensed by them within their jurisdiction, and for regulating the times during which they shall severally be allowed to be open; and from time to time, at another special session, of which notice shall be given as aforesaid, may rescind or alter such rules; and it shall be lawful for any one of her Majesty's principal Secretaries of State to rescind or alter any such rules, and also to make such other rules for the like purpose as to him shall seem fit; and a copy of all rules which shall be in force for the time being shall be annexed to every such licence; and in case any riot or breach of the said rules in any such theatre shall be proved on oath, before any two justices usually acting in the jurisdiction where such theatre is situated, it shall be lawful for them to order that the same be closed for such time as to the said justices shall seem fit; and while such order shall be in force, the theatre so ordered to be closed shall be deemed an unlicensed house.

Proviso for the Universities of Oxford and Cambridge.

10. Provided always and be it enacted, that no such licence shall be in force within the precincts of either of the universities of Oxford or Cambridge, or within fourteen miles of the city of Oxford or the town of Cambridge, without the consent of the Chancellor or Vice-Chancellor of each of the said universities respectively, and that the rules for the management of any theatre which shall be licensed with such consent within the limits aforesaid shall be subject to the approval of the said Chancellor or Vice-Chancellor respectively; and in case of a breach of any of the said rules, or of any condition on which the consent of the Chancellor or Vice-Chancellor to grant any such licence shall have been given, it shall be lawful for such Chancellor or Vice Chancellor respectively to annul the licence, and thereupon such licence shall become void.

Penalty on persons performing in unlicensed places.

11. And be it enacted, that every person, who for hire shall act or present, or cause, permit or suffer to be acted or presented any part in any stage-play in any place not being a patent theatre or duly licensed as a theatre, shall forfeit such sum as shall be awarded by the court in which, and the justices by whom he shall be convicted, not exceeding ten pounds for every day on which he shall so offend.

No new plays or additions to old ones to be acted until submitted to the Lord Chamberlain.

12. And be it enacted, that one copy of every new stage-play, and of every new act, scene, or other part added to any old stage-play, and of every new prologue or epilogue, and of every new part added to an old prologue or epilogue intended to be produced and acted for hire at any theatre in Great Britain, shall be sent to the Lord Chamberlain of her Majesty's household for the time being, seven days at least before the

first acting or presenting thereof, with an account of the theatre where, and the time when the same is intended to be first acted or presented, signed by the master or manager, or one of the masters or managers of such theatre; and during the said seven days no person shall, for hire, act or present the same, or cause the same to be acted or presented, and in case the Lord Chamberlain, either before or after the expiration of the said period of seven days, shall disallow any play, or any act, scene or part thereof, or any prologue or epilogue, or any part thereof, it shall not be lawful for any person to act or present the same, or cause the same to be acted or presented contrary to such disallowance.

13. And be it enacted, that it shall be lawful for the Lord Chamberlain to charge such fees for the examination of the plays, prologues and epilogues, or parts thereof, which shall be sent to him for examination, as to him from time to time shall seem fit, according to a scale which shall be fixed by him, such fee not being in any case more than two guineas, and such fees shall be paid at the time when such plays, prologues and epilogues, or parts thereof shall be sent to the Lord Chamberlain, and the said period of seven days shall not begin to run in any case until the said fee shall have been paid to the Lord Chamberlain, or to some officer deputed by him to receive the same. *Fees to be paid for examination of plays, &c.*

14. And be it enacted, that it shall be lawful for the Lord Chamberlain, for the time being, whenever he shall be of opinion that it is fitting for the preservation of good manners, decorum, or of the public peace so to do, to forbid the acting, or presenting any stage-play, or any act, scene or part thereof, or any prologue or epilogue, or any part thereof anywhere in Great Britain, or in such theatre as he shall specify, and either absolutely or for such time as he shall think fit. *The Lord Chamberlain may forbid any play.*

15. And be it enacted, that every person, who for hire shall act or present, or cause to be acted or presented, any new stage-play, or any act, scene, or part thereof, or any new prologue or epilogue, or any part thereof, until the same shall have been allowed by the Lord Chamberlain, or which shall have been disallowed by him; and also every person, who for hire shall act or present, or cause to be acted or presented, any stage-play, or any act, scene or part thereof, or any prologue or epilogue, or any part thereof, contrary to such prohibition as aforesaid, shall, for every such offence, forfeit such sum as shall be awarded by the court in which, or the justices by whom he shall be convicted, not exceeding the sum of fifty pounds, and every licence (in case there be any such), by or under which the theatre was opened, in which such offence shall have been committed, shall become absolutely void. *Penalty for acting plays before they are allowed or after they are disallowed.*

What shall be evidence of acting for hire.

16. And be it enacted, that in every case in which any money or other reward shall be taken or charged, directly or indirectly, or in which the purchase of any article is made a condition for the admission of any person into any theatre, to see any stage-play, and also in every case in which any stage-play shall be acted or presented in any house, room or place, in which distilled or fermented exciseable liquor shall be sold, every actor therein shall be deemed to be acting for hire.

Proof of licence in certain cases to lie on the party accused.

17. And be it enacted, that in any proceedings to be instituted against any person for having or keeping an unlicensed theatre, or for acting for hire in an unlicensed theatre, if it shall be proved that such theatre is used for the public performance of stage-plays, the burden of proof that such theatre is duly licensed or authorised shall lie on the party accused, and until the contrary shall be proved, such theatre shall be taken to be unlicensed.

18. [*Proceedings begun before the passing of this Act may be discontinued.*]

Penalties, how to be recoverable.

19. And be it enacted, that all the pecuniary penalties imposed by this Act for offences committed in England may be recovered in any of her Majesty's Courts of Record at Westminster; and for offences committed in Scotland, by action or summary complaint before the Court of Session or Justiciary there; or for offences committed in any part of Great Britain, in a summary way before two justices of the peace for any county, riding, division, liberty, city, or borough, where any such offence shall be committed, by the oath or oaths of one or more credible witness or witnesses, or by the confession of the offender; and in default of payment of such penalty together with the costs, the same may be levied by distress and sale of the offender's goods and chattels, rendering the overplus to such offender if any there be above the penalty, costs, and charge of distress; and for want of sufficient distress the offender may be imprisoned in the common gaol or house of correction of any such county, riding, division, liberty, city, or borough, for any time not exceeding six calendar months.

Appeal.

20. And be it enacted, that it shall be lawful for any person who shall think himself aggrieved by any order of such justices of the peace, to appeal therefrom to the next General or Quarter Session of the Peace to be holden for the said county, riding, division, liberty, city or borough, whose order thereon shall be final.

Appropriation of penalties.

21. And be it enacted, that the said penalties for any offence against this Act shall be paid and applied, in the first instance, toward defraying the expenses incurred by the prosecutor, and the residue thereof, if any, shall be paid to the use of her Majesty, her heirs and successors.

22. Provided always, and be it enacted, that no person shall be liable to be prosecuted for any offence against this Act unless such prosecution shall be commenced within six calendar months after the offence committed. *Limitation of actions.*

23. And be it enacted, that in this Act the word 'stage-play' shall be taken to include every tragedy, comedy, farce, opera, burletta, interlude, melodrama, pantomime, or other entertainment of the stage, or any part thereof. Provided always, that nothing herein contained shall be construed to apply to any theatrical representation in any booth or show which, by the justices of the peace, or other persons having authority in that behalf, shall be allowed in any lawful fair, feast, or customary meeting of the like kind. *Interpretation of Act.*

24. And be it enacted, that the Act shall extend only to Great Britain. *Limits of the Act.*

25. [*Power to amend the Act during the Session.*]

V. Statute 7 & 8 Vic. c. 12.

An Act to amend the Law relating to International Copyright.

[10 May 1844.]

Whereas, by an Act passed in the session of Parliament held in the first and second years of the reign of her present Majesty, intituled 'An Act for securing to authors, in certain cases, the benefit of international copyright (and which Act is hereinafter, for the sake of perspicuity, designated as The International Copyright Act,'), her Majesty was empowered by Order in Council to direct that the authors of books which should, after a future time to be specified in such Order in Council, be published in any foreign country to be specified in such Order in Council, and their executors, administrators, and assigns, should have the sole liberty of printing and reprinting such books within the British dominions, for such term as her Majesty should by such Order in Council direct, not exceeding the term which authors, being British subjects, were then (that is to say, at the time of passing the said Act) entitled to in respect of books first published in the United Kingdom; and the said Act contains divers enactments, securing to authors and their representatives the copyright in the books to which any such Order in Council should extend. And whereas an Act was passed in the session of Parliament held in the fifth and sixth years of the reign of her present Majesty, intituled 'An Act to amend the Law of Copyright' (and which Act is hereinafter, for the sake of perspicuity, designated as 'The Copyright Amendment Act'), repealing various Acts therein mentioned relating to the copyright of printed books, and extending, *1 & 2 Vic. c. 59.* *5 & 6 Vic. c. 45.*

defining, and securing to authors and their representatives the copyright of books.. And whereas an Act was passed in the session of Parliament held in the third and fourth years of the reign of his late Majesty King William the Fourth, intituled 'An Act to amend the Laws relating to Dramatic Literary Property' (and which Act is hereinafter, for the sake of perspicuity, designated as 'The Dramatic Literary Property Act'), whereby the sole liberty of representing, or causing to be represented, any dramatic piece in any place of dramatic entertainment in any part of the British dominions, which should be composed and not printed or published by the author thereof or his assignee, was secured to such author or his assignee; and by the said Act it was enacted that the author of any such production which should thereafter be printed and published, or his assignee, should have the like sole liberty of representation until the end of twenty-eight years from the first publication thereof; And whereas by the said Copyright Amendment Act, the provisions of the said Dramatic Literary Property Act, and of the said Copyright Amendment Act were made applicable to musical compositions; and it was thereby also enacted, that the sole liberty of representing or performing, or causing or permitting to be represented or performed, in any part of the British dominions, any dramatic piece or musical composition, should endure and be the property of the author thereof and his assigns, for the term in the said Copyright Amendment Act provided for the duration of the copyright in books, and that the provisions therein enacted in respect of the property of such copyright should apply to the liberty of representing or performing any dramatic piece or musical composition.

[*Here follow recitals of Acts relating to engravings, sculpture, and models.*]

And whereas the powers vested in her Majesty by the said International Copyright Act are insufficient to enable her Majesty to confer upon authors of books first published in foreign countries copyright of the like duration, and with the like remedies for the infringement thereof, which are conferred and provided by the said Copyright Amendment Act with respect to authors of books first published in the British dominions; and the said International Copyright Act does not empower her Majesty to confer any exclusive right of representing or performing dramatic pieces or musical compositions first published in foreign countries upon the authors thereof, nor to extend the privilege of copyright to prints and sculpture first published abroad; and it is expedient to vest increased powers in her Majesty in this respect, and for that purpose to repeal the said International Copyright Act, and to give such other powers to her Majesty, and to make such further provisions as are hereinafter contained: be it therefore enacted by the Queen's Most Excellent Majesty, by and with the advice and consent of the Lords Spiritual and Temporal, and Commons, in this present Parliament assembled, and by the authority of the same, that the said recited Act herein designated as the International Copyright Act, shall be, and the same is hereby repealed.

<small>Repeal of International Copyright Act.</small>

2. And be it enacted, that it shall be lawful for her Majesty, by any order of her Majesty in Council, to direct that, as respects all or any particular class or classes of the following works, namely, books, prints, articles of sculpture, and other works of art, to be defined in such order, which shall after a future time, to be specified in such order, be first published in any foreign country, to be named in such order, the authors, inventors, designers, engravers, and makers thereof respectively, their respective executors, administrators, and assigns, shall have the privilege of copyright therein during such period or respective periods as shall be defined in such order, not exceeding however, as to any of the above-mentioned works, the term of copyright which authors, inventors, designers, engravers, and makers of the like works respectively first published in the United Kingdom, may be then entitled to under the hereinbefore recited Acts respectively, or under any Acts which may hereafter be passed in that behalf.

<small>Her Majesty, by order in Council, may direct that authors, &c., of works first published in foreign countries shall have copyright therein within her Majesty's dominions.</small>

3. And be it enacted, that in case any such order shall apply to books, all and singular the enactments of the said Copyright Amendment Act, and of any other Act for the time being in force with relation to the copyright in books first published in this country, shall from and after the time so to be specified in that behalf in such order, and subject to such limitation as to the duration of the copyright as shall be therein contained, apply to and be in force in respect of the books to which such order shall extend, and which shall have been registered as hereinafter is provided, in such and the same manner as if such books were first published in the United Kingdom: save and except such of the said enactments or such parts thereof as shall be excepted in such order, and save and except such of the said enactments as relate to the delivery of copies of books at the British Museum, and to or for the use of the other libraries mentioned in the said Copyright Amendment Act.

<small>If the order applies to books, the Copyright Law as to books first published in this country shall apply to the books to which the order relates, with certain exceptions.</small>

4. (*If the order applies to prints, sculptures, &c., the Copyright Law as to prints or sculptures first published in this country, shall apply to the prints, sculptures, &c., to which such order relates.*)

5. And be it enacted, that it shall be lawful for her Majesty, by any order of her Majesty in Council, to direct that the authors of dramatic pieces and musical compositions, which

<small>Her Majesty may by Order in Council</small>

direct that authors and composers of dramatic pieces and musical compositions first publicly represented and performed in foreign countries shall have similar rights in the British dominions.

shall after a future time, to be specified in such order, be first publicly represented or performed in any foreign country, to be named in such order, shall have the sole liberty of representing or performing in any part of the British Dominions such dramatic pieces or musical compositions during such period as shall be defined in such order, not exceeding the period during which authors of dramatic pieces and musical compositions first publicly represented or performed in the United Kingdom, may for the time be entitled by law to the sole liberty of representing and performing the same; and from and after the time so specified in any such last-mentioned order the enactments of the said Dramatic Literary Property Act, and of the said Copyright Amendment Act, and of any other Act, for the time being in force with relation to the liberty of publicly representing and performing dramatic pieces or musical compositions, shall, subject to such limitation as to the duration of the right conferred by any such order as shall be therein contained, apply to and be in force in respect of the dramatic pieces and musical compositions to which such order shall extend, and which shall have been registered as hereinafter is provided, in such and the same manner as if such dramatic pieces and musical compositions had been first publicly represented and performed in the British dominions, save and except such of the said enactments or such parts thereof as shall be excepted in such order.

Particulars to be observed as to registry, and to delivery of copies.

6. Provided always and be it enacted, that no author of any book, dramatic piece, or musical composition, or his executors, administrators, or assigns, and no inventor, designer, or engraver of any print, or maker of any article of sculpture, or other work of art, his executors, administrators, or assigns, shall be entitled to the benefit of this Act, or of any Order in Council to be issued in pursuance thereof, unless within a time or times to be in that behalf prescribed in each such Order in Council, such book, dramatic piece, musical composition, print, article of sculpture, or other work of art shall have been so registered, and such copy thereof shall have been so delivered as hereinafter is mentioned (that is to say): as regards such book, and also such dramatic piece or musical composition (in the event of the same having been printed), the title to the copy thereof, the name and place of abode of the author or composer thereof, the name and place of abode of the proprietor of the copyright thereof, the time and place of the first publication, representation, or performance thereof, as the case may be in the foreign country named in the Order in Council under which the benefits of this Act shall be claimed, shall be entered in the register-book of the Company of Stationers in London, and one printed copy of the whole

of such book, and of such dramatic piece or musical composition (in the event of the same having been printed) and or every volume thereof, upon the best paper upon which the largest number or impression of the book, dramatic piece, or musical composition, shall have been printed for sale, together with all maps and prints relating thereto, shall be delivered to the officer of the Company of Stationers at the Hall of the said Company; and as regards dramatic pieces and musical compositions in manuscript, the title to the same, the name and place of abode of the author or composer thereof, the name and place of abode of the proprietor of the right of representing or performing the same, and the time and place of the first representation or performance thereof in the country named in the Order in Council under which the benefit of the Act shall be claimed, shall be entered in the said register-book of the said Company of Stationers in London . . .

(*Provisions with regard to prints, sculptures, &c.*)

. . . and the officer of the said Company of Stationers receiving such copies so to be delivered as aforesaid, shall give a receipt in writing for the same, and such delivery shall to all intents and purposes be a sufficient delivery under the provisions of this Act.

7. [*In case of books published anonymously, the name of the publisher to be sufficient.*]

8. And be it enacted, that the several enactments in the said Copyright Amendment Act contained with relation to keeping the said register-book and the inspection thereof, the searches therein, and the delivery of certified and stamped copies thereof, the reception of such copies in evidence, the making of false entries in the said book, and the production in evidence of papers falsely purporting to be copies of entries in the said book, the application to the Courts and Judges by persons aggrieved by entries in the said book, and the expunging and varying such entries, shall apply to the books, dramatic pieces and musical compositions, prints, articles of sculpture, and other works of art to which any Order in Council, issued in pursuance of this Act shall extend, and to the entries and assignments of copyright and proprietorship therein, in such and the same manner as if such enactments were here expressly enacted in relation thereto, save and except that the forms of entry prescribed by the said Copyright Amendment Act may be varied to meet the circumstances of the case, and that the sum to be demanded by the officer of the said Company of Stationers for making any entry required by this Act shall be one shilling only. *The provisions of the Copyright Amendment Act as regards entries in the register book of the Company of Stationers, &c., to apply to entries under this Act.*

9. And be it enacted, that every entry made in pursuance of this Act of a first publication shall be *primâ facie* proof of a *As to expunging or varying en-*

try grounded in wrongful first publication.

rightful first publication; but if there be a wrongful first publication, and any party have availed himself thereof to obtain an entry of a spurious work, no order for expunging or varying such entry shall be made, unless it be proved to the satisfaction of the Court, or of the judge taking cognizance of the application for expunging or varying such entry; first, with respect to a wrongful publication in a country to which the author or first publisher does not belong, and in regard to which there does not subsist with this country any treaty of international copyright, that the party making the application was the author or first publisher, as the case requires; second, with respect to a wrongful first publication, either in the country where a rightful first publication has taken place, or in regard to which there subsists with this country a treaty of international copyright, that a Court of competent jurisdiction in any such country where such wrongful first publication has taken place has given judgment in favour of the right of the party claiming to be the author or first publisher.

Copies of books wherein copyright is subsisting under this Act printed in foreign countries other than those wherein the book was first published prohibited to be imported.

10. And be it enacted, that all copies of books wherein there shall be any subsisting copyright under or by virtue of this Act, or of any Order in Council made in pursuance thereof, printed or reprinted in any foreign country, except that in which such books were first published, shall be, and the same are hereby absolutely prohibited to be imported into any part of the British dominions, except by or with the consent of the registered proprietor of the copyright thereof, or his agent authorised in writing; and if imported contrary to this prohibition, the same, and the importers thereof, shall be subject to the enactments in force relating to goods prohibited to be imported by any Act relating to the Customs, and as respects any such copies so prohibited to be imported, and also as respects any copies unlawfully printed in any place whatsoever of any books wherein there shall be any such subsisting copyright as aforesaid, any person who shall, in any part of the British dominions, import such prohibited or unlawfully printed copies, or who, knowing such copies to be so unlawfully imported or unlawfully printed, shall sell, publish, or expose to sale or hire, or shall cause to be sold, published, or exposed to sale or hire, or have in his possession for sale or hire, any such copies so unlawfully imported or unlawfully printed, such offender shall be liable to a special action on the case, at the suit of the proprietor of such copyright, to be brought and prosecuted in the same Courts, and in the same manner, and with the like restrictions upon the proceedings of the defendant, as are respectively prescribed in the said Copyright Amendment Act, with relation to actions thereby authorised to be brought by proprietors of copyright against persons importing or selling books unlawfully printed in the British dominions.

STATUTE 7 & 8 VIC. C. 12.   xlv

11. [*Officer of Stationers' Company to deposit books, &c., in the British Museum.*]

12. [*Proviso as to second or subsequent editions.*]

13. [*Orders in Council may specify different periods for different foreign countries and for different classes of works.*]

14. Provided always, and be it enacted, that no such Order in Council shall have any effect unless it shall be therein stated as the ground for issuing the same, that due protection has been secured by the foreign power so named in such Order in Council for the benefit of parties interested in works first published in the dominions of her Majesty, similar to those comprised in such orders. *No Order in Council to have any effect unless it states that reciprocal protection is secured.*

15. And be it enacted, that every Order in Council to be made under the authority of this Act, shall, as soon as may be after this making thereof by her Majesty in Council, be published in the 'London Gazette,' and from the time of such publication shall have the same effect as if every part thereof were included in this Act. *Order in Council to be published in Gazette and to have same effect as this Act.*

16. And be it enacted, that a copy of every Order of her Majesty in Council made under this Act shall be laid before both Houses of Parliament within six weeks after issuing the same, if Parliament be then sitting; and if not, then within six weeks after the commencement of the then next session of Parliament. *Orders in Council to be laid before Parliament.*

17. And be it enacted, that it shall be lawful for her Majesty by an Order in Council, from time to time to revoke or alter any Order in Council previously made under the authority of this Act, but, nevertheless, without prejudice to any rights acquired previously to such revocation or alteration. *Orders in Council may be revoked.*

18. [Provided always, and be it enacted, that nothing in this Act contained shall be construed to prevent the printing, publication or sale, of any translation of any book, the author whereof, and his assigns, may be entitled to the benefit of this Act, *Repealed by* 15 & 16 Vict. c. 12, s. 1.] *Translations.*

19. And be it enacted, that neither the author of any book, nor the author or composer of any dramatic piece or musical composition, nor the inventor, designer, or engraver of any print, nor the maker of any article of sculpture, or of such other work of art, as aforesaid, which shall, after the passing of this Act, be first published out of her Majesty's dominions, shall have any copyright therein respectively, or any exclusive right to the public representation or performance thereof, otherwise than such (if any) as he may become entitled to under this Act. *Authors of works first published in foreign countries not entitled to copyright except under this Act.*

20. And be it enacted, that in the construction of this Act, the word 'book' shall be construed to include volume, pamphlet, sheet of letter-press, sheet of music, map, chart or plan; and the expression, 'articles of sculpture' shall mean all such *Interpretation clauses.*

sculptures, models, copies and casts, as are described in the said Sculpture Copyright Acts, and in respect of which the privileges of Copyright are thereby conferred; and the words, 'printing and reprinting,' shall include engraving, and any other method of multiplying copies; and the expression, 'her Majesty,' shall include the heirs and successors of her Majesty; and the expressions 'Order of her Majesty in Council,' 'Order in Council,' and 'Order,' shall respectively mean, Order of her Majesty acting by and with the advice of her Majesty's most honourable Privy Council; and the expression, 'Officer of the Company of Stationers,' shall mean the officer appointed by the said Company of Stationers for the purposes of the said Copyright Amendment Act; and in describing any persons or things, any word importing the plural number, shall mean also one person or thing, and any word importing the singular number, shall include several persons or things, and any word importing the masculine shall include also the feminine gender, unless in any of such cases there shall be something in the subject or context repugnant to such construction.

Act may be repealed this Session. 21. And be it enacted, that this Act may be amended or repealed by any Act to be passed in this present session of Parliament.

VI. STATUTE 15 & 16 Vic., cap. 12.

An Act to enable her Majesty to carry into effect a Convention with France on the subject of Copyright; to extend and explain the International Copyright Acts; and to explain the Acts relating to Copyright in Engravings.

[May 28, 1852.]

Whereas an Act was passed in the seventh year of the reign of her present Majesty [7 & 8 Vic. c. 12] intituled An Act to amend the Law relating to International Copyright hereinafter called 'The International Copyright Act,' and whereas a convention has lately been concluded between her Majesty and the French Republic for extending in each country the enjoyment of copyright in works of literature, and the fine arts first published in the other, and for certain reductions of duties now levied on books, prints, and musical works published in France; and whereas certain of the stipulations on the part of her Majesty contained in the said treaty require the authority of Parliament, and whereas it is expedient that such authority should be given, and that her Majesty should be enabled to make similar stipulations in any treaty on the subject of copyright which may hereafter be concluded with any foreign power, be it enacted &c. as follows:—

Partial re- Section 1. The 18th section of the said Act of the seventh

STATUTE 15 & 16 VIC. c. 12.   xlvii

year of her present Majesty, chapter twelve, shall be repealed so far as the same is inconsistent with the provisions hereinafter contained.

peal of 7 & 8 Vic. c. 18.

2. Her Majesty may, by Order in Council, direct that the authors of books which are, after a future time to be specified in such order, published in any foreign country to be named in such order, their executors, administrators, and assigns shall, subject to the provisions hereinafter contained or referred to, be empowered to prevent the publication in the British dominions of any translations of such books not authorised by them, for such time as may be specified in such order, not extending beyond the expiration of five years from the time at which the authorised translations of such books hereinafter mentioned are respectively first published, and in the case of books published in parts not extending, as to each part, beyond the expiration of five years from the time at which the authorised translation of such part is first published.

Her Majesty may by Order in Council direct that authors of books published in foreign countries may for a limited time prevent unauthorised translations.

3. Subject to any provisions or qualifications contained in such order, and to the provisions herein-contained or referred to, the laws and enactments for the time being in force for the purpose of preventing the infringement of copyright in books published in the British dominions shall be applied for the purpose of preventing the publication of translations of the books to which such order extends, which are not sanctioned by the authors of such books, except only such parts of the said enactments as relate to the delivery of copies of books for the use of the British Museum, and for the use of the other libraries therein referred to.

Thereupon the law of copyrights shall extend to prevent such translations.

4. Her Majesty may, by Order in Council, direct that authors of dramatic pieces which are, after a future time, to be specified in such order, first publicly represented in any foreign country, to be named in such order, their executors, administrators and assigns, shall, subject to the provisions hereinafter mentioned or referred to, be empowered to prevent the representation in the British dominions of any translation of such dramatic pieces not authorised by them, for such time as may be specified in such order, not extending beyond the expiration of five years from the time at which the authorised translations of such dramatic pieces hereinafter mentioned are first published or publicly represented.

Her Majesty may by Order in Council direct that the authors of dramatic works represented in foreign countries may for a limited time prevent unauthorised translations.

5. Subject to any provisions or qualifications contained in such last-mentioned order, and to the provisions hereinafter contained or referred to, the laws and enactments for the time being in force for insuring to the author of any dramatic piece first publicly represented in the British dominions the sole liberty of representing the same shall be applied for the purpose of preventing the representation of any translations of the dramatic pieces to which such last-mentioned order extends, which are not sanctioned by the authors thereof.

Thereupon the law for protecting the representation of such pieces shall extend to prevent unauthorised translations.

Adaptations, &c. of dramatic pieces to the English stage not prevented.

6. Nothing herein contained shall be so construed as to prevent fair imitations or adaptations to the English stage of any dramatic piece or musical composition published in any foreign country.

All articles in newspapers, &c. relating to politics may be republished or translated, and also all similar articles on any subject, unless the author has notified his intention to reserve the right.

7. Notwithstanding anything in the said International Copyright Act, or in this Act contained, any article of political discussion which has been published in any newspaper or periodical in a foreign country, may, if the source from which the same is taken be acknowledged, be republished or translated in any newspaper or periodical in this country, and any article relating to any other subject which has been so published as aforesaid, may, if the source from which the same is taken be acknowledged, be republished or translated in like manner, unless the author has signified his intention of preserving the copyright therein and the right of translating the same in some conspicuous part of the newspaper or periodical in which the same was first published, in which case the same shall, without the formalities required by the next following section, receive the same protection as is by virtue of the International Copyright Act or this Act extended to books.

No author to be entitled to benefit of this Act without complying with the requisitions herein specified.

8. No author or his executors, administrators or assigns, shall be entitled to the benefit of this Act, or of any Order in Council issued in pursuance thereof in respect of the translation of any book or dramatic piece if the following requisitions are not complied with, that is to say—

(1). The original work from which the translation is to be made must be registered, and a copy thereof deposited in the United Kingdom, in the manner required for original works by the said International Copyright Act, within three calendar months of its first publication in the foreign country.

(2). The author must notify on the title page of the original work, or if it is published in parts on the title page of the first part, or if there is no title page on some conspicuous part of the work that it is his intention to reserve the right of translating it.

(3). The translation sanctioned by the author or a part thereof must be published either in the country mentioned in the Order in Council by virtue of which it is to be protected, or in the British dominions not later than one year after the registration and deposit in the United Kingdom of the original work, and the whole of such translation must be published within three years of such registration and deposit.

(4.) Such translation must be registered, and a copy thereof deposited in the United Kingdom, within a time to be mentioned in that behalf in the order by which it is protected, and in the manner provided by the said International Copyright Act for the registration and deposit of original works.

(5.) In the case of books published in parts, each part of the original work must be registered and deposited in this country, in the manner required by the said International Copyright Act, within three months after the first publication thereof in the foreign country.

(6.) In the case of dramatic pieces, the translation sanctioned by the author must be published within three calendar months of the registration of the original work.

(7.) The above requisitions shall apply to articles originally published in newspapers or periodicals, if the same be afterwards published in a separate form, but shall not apply to such articles as originally published.

9. All copies of any works of literature or art, wherein there is any subsisting copyright by virtue of the International Copyright Act and this Act, or of any Order in Council made in pursuance of such Acts or either of them, and which are printed, reprinted, or made in any foreign country, except that in which such work shall be first published, and all unauthorised translations of any book or dramatic piece, the publication or public representation in the British dominions of translations whereof, not authorised as in this Act mentioned, shall for the time being be prevented under any Order in Council made in pursuance of this Act, are hereby absolutely prohibited to be imported into any part of the British dominions, except by or with the consent of the registered proprietor of the copyright of such work, or of such book or piece, or his agent, authorised in writing; and the provisions of the Act of the sixth year of her Majesty [5 & 6 Vic. c. 45], 'To amend the Law of Copyright,' for the forfeiture, seizure, and destruction of any printed book first published in the United Kingdom wherein there shall be copyright, and reprinted in any country out of the British dominions and imported into any part of the British dominions by any person not being the proprietor of the copyright, or a person authorised by such proprietor, shall extend and be applicable to all copies of any works of literature and art, and to all translations, the importation whereof into any part of the British dominions is prohibited under this Act.

Pirated copies prohibited to be imported except with consent of proprietor.

Provisions of 5 & 6 Vic. c. 45 as to forfeiture, &c. of pirated works, &c. to extend to works prohibited to be imported under this Act.

10. The provisions hereinbefore contained shall be incorporated with the International Act, and shall be read and construed therewith as one Act.

Foregoing provisions and 7 & 8 Vic. c. 12 to be read as one Act.

11. And whereas her Majesty has already, by Order in Council under the said International Copyright Act, given effect to certain stipulations contained in the said convention with the French Republic; and it is expedient that the remainder of the stipulations on the part of her Majesty in the said convention contained should take effect from the passing of this Act without any further Order in Council during the continuance of the said convention, and so long as the Order in Council already made under the said International

French translations to be protected as herein before mentioned without further Order in Council.

APPENDIX.

Copyright Act remains in force, the provisions hereinbefore contained shall apply to the said convention, and to translations of books and dramatic pieces which are, after the passing of this Act, published or represented in France, in the same manner as if her Majesty had issued her Order in Council in pursuance of this Act for giving effect to such convention, and had therein directed that such translations should be protected, as hereinbefore mentioned, for a period of five years from the date of the first publication or public representation thereof respectively, and as if a period of three months from the publication of such translation were the time mentioned in such order, as the time within which the same must be registered, and a copy thereof deposited in the United Kingdom.

(*The remaining sections of this Act refer to the reduction of duties, lithographs, prints, &c.*)

Orders in Council.

Copy of an Order of her Majesty in Council directing that French Authors, &c., shall have the privilege of Copyright.

AT the Court at Windsor, the 10th day of January, 1852, Present, The Queen's Most Excellent Majesty in Council.

Whereas a treaty has been concluded between her Majesty and the President of the French Republic, whereby due protection has been secured within the French dominions for the authors of books, dramatic works, musical compositions, drawings, paintings, sculpture, engravings, lithographs, and any other works of literature and of the fine arts, in which the laws of Great Britain and of France do now or may hereafter give their respective subjects the right of property or copyright, and for the lawful representatives or assigns of such authors with regard to any such works first published within the dominions of her Majesty.

Now therefore, her Majesty, by and with the advice and consent of her Privy Council, and by virtue of the authority committed to her by an Act passed in the Session of Parliament holden in the seventh and eighth years of her reign, intituled 'An Act to amend the Law relating to International Copyright,' doth order, and it is hereby ordered, that from and after the 17th day of January, 1852, the authors, inventors, designers, engravers, and makers of any of the following works, (that is to say), books, prints, articles of sculpture, dramatic works, musical compositions, and any other works of literature and the fine arts in which the laws of Great Britain give to British subjects the privilege of copyright, and the executors, administrators, and assigns of such authors, inventors, designers, engravers, and makers respectively shall, as respects works first published within the dominions of France after the said 17th day of January, 1852, have the privilege of copyright therein for a period equal to the term of copyright, which authors, inventors, designers, engravers, and makers of the like works respectively first published in the United Kingdom are by law entitled to, provided such books, dramatic pieces, musical compositions, prints, articles of sculpture, or other works of art have been registered, and copies thereof have been delivered according to the requirements of the said recited Act within three months after the first publication thereof in any part of the French dominions, or if such work be published in parts, then within three months after the publication of the last part thereof. And it is hereby further ordered, that the authors of dramatic pieces and musical compositions which shall after the said 17th day of January, 1852, be first publicly represented or performed within the dominions of France, or their assignees, shall have the sole liberty of representing or performing in any part of the British dominions such dramatic pieces or musical compositions during a period equal to the period during which authors of dramatic pieces and musical compositions first publicly represented or performed in the United Kingdom, or their assignees are entitled by law to the sole liberty of representing or performing the same, provided such dramatic pieces or musical compositions have been registered, and copies thereof have been delivered according to the requirements of the said recited Act within three months after the time of their being first represented or performed in any part of the French dominions.

And the Right Honourable the Lords Commissioners of her Majesty's Treasury are to give the necessary directions herein accordingly.

(Signed) WM. L. BATHURST.

An Order of Council of the same date reduces the duties on books, prints, and drawings published in the dominions of France.

Similar Orders have been issued with reference to other States with which international conventions have been concluded.

www.ingramcontent.com/pod-product-compliance
Lightning Source LLC
Chambersburg PA
CBHW030312170426
43202CB00009B/970